Mother Imagined

Mother Imagined

A Personal Journey:
Learning to Let Go of My Toxic Mother

Reason Carmichael

PALMETTO
PUBLISHING
Charleston, SC
www.PalmettoPublishing.com

This book is lovingly dedicated to…

My husband, Terry, and my son, Blake, whose undying love and unending support have saved my life over and over again in so many ways they will never know. I love them both to the moon and back.

My brother, Brad, who was always there to pick up the pieces for me during our growing-up years. I love him and wouldn't have made it without him.

My therapist, Amber, for guiding me on my path of healing. Her kind validation and support have been invaluable and have also helped save my life.

My very best friends who have walked this path with me at varying times in my life: Alisha, Heather, Jennifer, and Robin.

Table of Contents

Preface. ix

Chapter One: My Constant Question—Why? 1

Chapter Two: My Childhood Years. 15

Chapter Three: My Teenage and College Years 23

Chapter Four: My Wedding .36

Chapter Five: My Early Career Years. 50

Chapter Six: My Son's Arrival 57

Chapter Seven: My Adult to Middle-Age Years 66

Chapter Eight: My Periods of Estrangement from Mom . . .77

Chapter Nine: My Last Experience with Mom. 84

Chapter Ten: My Happy Memories 90

Chapter Eleven: My Healing Journey. 95

References. 109

About the Author 111

Preface

If you were intrigued by the title of this book and find yourself reading this page, you have likely been through, or are currently experiencing, a journey similar to my own. It could also be that it's not your own personal journey, but it's someone you know who finds herself in the midst of a madness much like I've experienced. It is difficult to describe, but I think the time has come for me to try. The mother I've always hoped for, my "mother imagined," is the one whose warm and loving voice I hear when she realizes it's me on the phone, and the one whose heart is happy when she observes my happiness. It's not so with my mother, and I've only recently realized that this fantasy I've held about her is all in my imagination, which is extremely difficult to digest.

The mother I've always imagined is happy to be with me, celebrates my successes, and loves me unconditionally. She gives me grace and shows me empathy when needed, always letting me know she's there for me no matter what. My "mother imagined" checks in on me and asks me how my day was, or how an interview went, or the status of a specific project at work that I had mentioned. She tells me how proud she is of me and makes me feel that she only wants the best for me. I imagine hearing joy in her voice when I answer her phone call, not disdain or disgust. These ruminations in my mind are only fiction, however, because my mother is none of these things. Sherrie Campbell describes it best when she writes, "We erroneously believe that if we try to be good enough, successful, or perfect, maybe our toxic family members will change their minds about us. But they don't and they won't" (2019, 107). What a true statement indeed! It has taken me over four decades to realize that my "mother imagined" is simply a figment of my imagination and not real in any way, even though I had hoped for many years that she would one day materialize. I kept thinking that she would get better, but no matter what I did, things did not change.

I feel compelled to share my story as part of my own healing process, but also in hopes that it will prove meaningful to others who find themselves going down the same path. Although I am not a writer by trade, I hope my writing skills are sufficient to share my story in a careful and intentional way. Dysfunction tends to travel a spiral path and perpetuates itself from generation to generation, unless of course someone decides to stop its destructive forward locomotion. If a sufficient support system is in place and resources are available, I believe the progression of such dysfunction can be stopped. That is precisely what has brought me to this very moment in my life.

Most people grow up with some level of family dysfunction. We humans are flawed and often struggle as we navigate our complicated relationships. For me, the main source of this family dysfunction was my mother, who remains undiagnosed but for years has demonstrated behaviors that in my opinion most align with borderline personality disorder, or BPD. Anxiety and depression have been a part of her life since childhood from what I understand. She may also suffer from another type of personality disorder as I can describe a minimum of three distinct personalities based on my observations of her behavior. She has a Jekyll-and-Hyde personality that can change in an instant, much like the verbal attack called "the turn," as described by Christine Lawson in her book *Understanding The Borderline Mother*: "The turn is a sudden attack, the abrupt withdrawal of love and affection, and razor-sharp words that can pierce the heart as painfully as an arrow" (2000, 133). I have been on the receiving end of this sudden and often traumatic "turn" more times than I can even remember. When it happens, she actually looks possessed, as if she has become another person entirely, and it creates in me a primal fear that I don't have the words to describe. The forty-eight-hour period after such an experience elicits a zombielike state for me, which I've come to understand as a type of posttraumatic stress where I remain so shell shocked by her hateful behavior toward me that I simply go throughout my day like a robot or someone in a trance. "The turn reverses the mother-child relationship from one of loving acceptance to life-threatening rejection." The child that the mother "chooses to target feels annihilated after the turn" (Lawson 2000, 134). I know precisely what that annihilation feels like.

I received the last "turn" from my mother in April of 2022, and within a few days a close friend suggested I try talking to her therapist. I was reluctant to do so because I didn't think anyone would be able to help with my situation as it is far deeper than your run-of-the-mill mother-daughter conflict. After explaining my plight and grilling the therapist over email to explain that this was not just the typical mother-daughter relationship, I thought I would try talking with her; she assured me she could help. It was then that I started my journey of healing, which would lead to real progress in finally separating from my mom. In addition, I now know that the "turn" I experienced with her in 2022 would be the final one. I'm now learning to reorganize past experiences with her so I can recall them when needed without such intense pain and also continue healing my psychological and emotional wounds. I recognize that my journey has no real ending point, and that it's not a neat and clean, linear process where I move forward as I master each step. Instead, it's a completely spiral process where my brain replays conversations and experiences over and over again, the ones I can actually recall. Undoubtedly, it's a journey I'll continue on some level for the rest of my life.

CHAPTER ONE

My Constant Question—Why?

My depth of understanding with regard to my toxic mother has grown exponentially through my own research, reading, sessions with my therapist, and support from family and select close friends. The "mother imagined" in the depths of my soul is not at all like the one I actually have in real life, and I've just recently come to accept that fact. Even so, the young child in me (Little Girl Self), as my therapist has taught me, still wonders *why*. Why is she my mother? Why did she treat me in such a hateful way? Why didn't she care enough to try to get better? Why couldn't she just love me? Why did this happen to me? Now that I'm in my middle-age years, my therapist is helping me learn to let the adult in me (Big Girl Self) take the lead when my Little Girl Self feels brokenhearted over and over again.

There are four books that were life changing for me and pivotal in my journey of learning, healing, and acceptance. I'd be remiss if I didn't list them specifically here:

- *Stop Walking on Eggshells*, by Paul T. Mason and Randi Kreger, 2nd ed., 2010
- *Understanding The Borderline Mother*, by Christine Ann Lawson, PhD, 2000
- *But It's Your Family: Cutting Ties with Toxic Family Members and Loving Yourself in the Aftermath*, by Sherrie Campbell, PhD, 2019
- *What My Bones Know*, by Stephanie Foo, 2022

I actually read *Stop Walking on Eggshells* in 2007 and again in 2022 after the last verbal attack from my mom, and I did the same with *Understanding The Borderline Mother*. These two books, as well as the other two listed above, have played a critical role in my healing journey because they provided concrete validation of my experiences with my mother. They actually helped me see that I'm not crazy or lacking in some way, and that the situation with her really was emotionally abusive and far from normal. I've read other books and articles that were helpful as well, but these four remain the most meaningful to me.

No matter how much reading I complete, however, I will never understand why my mother is the way she is. My therapist reminds me that we cannot make sense of something that just doesn't make sense, although our brains are hardwired to figure things out and understand the reasons why things happen. Indeed, none of us can "make sense of chaos," as the authors of *Stop Walking on Eggshells* explain when describing borderline personality disorder in chapter 3 (Mason and Kreger 2010, 49–66). I wish I had written down more of my experiences with my mom so that I could remember details that I have long since forgotten or maybe never really captured to begin with. Since I didn't document every encounter with her, I created a timeline document where I've listed more specific information, but sometimes there are gaps of five years or more, and I don't have much information about those times.

For decades I thought my mother's behaviors were simply normal reactions to external factors, and I was very adept at justifying her behavior to others with this erroneous rationalization. I remember telling people that my mother has "had more stress and difficulties in life than other people do," which was just part of my fierce dedication to her as I kept pushing forward, defending her and earnestly thinking she'd get better. She had experienced the aforementioned family dysfunction, sadness from losing her dad when she was eighteen, divorce from my dad, returning to the workforce as a single mother, remarriage and acquiring grown stepchildren, breast cancer, a suicide attempt, and significant financial stress. Many other people have dealt with those same challenges, of course, but I always thought my mom had it worse than everyone else. In my mind, my "mother imagined" was simply trying to put the pieces back together for a return to some level of sanity, but of course that was not so. I could usually explain her behaviors and reactions because most of them seemed typical of other people who were going through the same life challenges. For many years I waited for circumstances in her life to align such that she would actually be happy, which of course never happened. Once I started junior high school (seventh grade) in 1981, I have no memory of my mother ever being happy. Alas, my "mother imagined" was only a figure in my fantasies that had no basis whatsoever in actual reality.

PICTURE OF ME IN 1981, AGE TWELVE

My therapist has helped me realize that one coping mechanism of mine has been dissociation, or as I put it, just forcing my thoughts and feelings into a box far in the back recesses of my brain—disconnecting myself mentally, so to speak. I became quite accomplished at this as a young adult, and it allowed me to focus on my career in education and not dwell on the craziness that was going on. I got very good at dissociating indeed. As Stephanie Foo explains, "In some moments of intense stress, we are super-duper good at dissociation" (2022, 310). Earlier in her book, she describes her own dissociation when dealing with her mother, and this passage really resonates with me: "If I took up all that space with my feelings, what space could I maintain for hers? Hers were more important. Because hers had greater stakes" (Foo 2022, 14). The mother I've imagined would help me work through my thoughts and feelings while validating my experiences without criticism. The mother of my reality, however, would immediately shift the focus to herself, her life, and her emotional state, since she believes that her stresses are always far worse than mine. "When you share something about yourself with such people, they immediately turn the account into a story about them" (Campbell 2019, 2).

I'm certain my mother experienced trauma as a child herself, and her parents separated in the early 1960s when she was in high school. They never divorced but remained separated until her father's death in March of 1965, during the spring semester of her freshman year in college. He had been a tail gunner in World War II and survived his plane being shot down and crash landing in a friendly Chinese village. None of us will ever know what hellish things he saw and experienced during that time. Like many young men in those days, he likely suffered what we now know as posttraumatic stress disorder (PTSD) but arrived home with expectations that he fall back into a "normal" routine with work, family, and related husband and father responsibilities. Alcohol was a way to numb his pain, and he became an alcoholic. From what I understand, however, he was not violent and mean when intoxicated as some people tend to be.

Everything I know about my paternal grandfather is that he was kind and unassuming, always showing love and affection to his three children, while my grandmother was more of the taskmaster. He died before I was born, so I never knew him, but based on what my mother always told me, he was her favorite parent. She related far better to him than her mother, and he spent time with her, always patiently describing new life experiences to her. The alcohol abuse that consumed him after the war was one of the things that jeopardized his marriage to my grandmother. At that time separation and divorce were rare, so it's likely my mother had no friends who understood what she was going through. She was the oldest of three who was expected to help put dinner on the table and manage things at home while my grandmother was juggling work and three children as a single mom. I believe my mother still harbors anger toward her own mother for the expectations placed on her during that time.

My mother once described to me a time when her father came home intoxicated, and my grandmother asked her to stand over him while holding a baseball bat in case he dared to stand up again and leave the house, which of course would cause shame and embarrassment to the family. I couldn't believe this had actually happened, and I felt so awful for my mom when she told me. I'm certain this situation was very traumatic for her to say the least, and I can't imagine that she ever "got over it," nor is it likely she was even allowed to talk through her feelings about it, which is terrible and so unhealthy, but typical at that time. This particular situation, as well as others I will never know about, created in her an intense anger toward her mother, which continued for the rest of my grandmother's life. Even after my grandmother's death in June of 2017, my mother often related events to me by referring to her as her "stupid mother."

This may sound surprising, but I remember life with Mom being pretty good during my early childhood years. When we moved to North Carolina during my second-grade year, though, I think she became very depressed, which affected her behavior toward my brother, Brad, and me. Things really changed for the worse, however, when I became a young adolescent, growing taller than she and looking more like an adult. Christine Lawson describes this shift when she explains the dependence of infants and young children and the reaction of a toxic mother who is losing control as her child is growing up: "As the child becomes increasingly independent, conflict erupts" (2000, 40). I'm learning now that this specific time period was more significant than I ever before realized, because I was approaching the teenage years but also perhaps because of what Dr. Campbell describes as she reflects on her own parents and her experiences as a clinical psychologist: "I have come to believe that toxic parents never wanted adult children. Instead they wanted dependent infants" (2019, 105). Maybe that is one reason things seemed to deteriorate so quickly once I was in seventh grade?

This was also the time when my parents separated, and my mother became a single parent about to enter the workforce after years of being a stay-at-home mom. Although she seemed glad that Dad was gone, she was under more stress being on her own with two kids and was likely dealing with increased depression that had never been treated. It's possible that my memories of her during my childhood are mainly good because she could play the role of Mommy as her two young children needed her for everything in life: food, baths, story time, and walks around the block. In other words, she was in control of all situations as my brother and I weren't yet old enough to have any real opinions of our own or do anything for ourselves.

My mom was always critical of others around her, making comments about people who were overweight or who, in her opinion, were lacking manners. She was very hard on herself as well and always sought perfection in all that she did. While it was the norm for her to be critical of everyone in her presence, once I started junior high, the focus of her wrath was usually me. If she saw me getting a snack in the kitchen, she would say, "You wear it well" with the most sarcastic tone of voice and a look of severe disapproval. Then she would remind me what she weighed when she was my age, how her shoe size was smaller than mine, and how petite her frame is. She constantly compared my life with hers and told me many times that I would make all of the mistakes she had made in her life, which I thought was so bizarre.

Often she looked at me with disdain in her eyes, like she actually hated me. At that time, I honestly started to fear her. As Sherrie Campbell describes, "We learn the hard way that no matter how much we love them, serve them, try our hardest for them, change ourselves, succeed, and so on, what we do will never be enough. They will not love us in return. They view our efforts toward pleasing them with a sense of contempt because they're consumed with jealousy and envy. They don't want to see us doing well or being good people" (2019, 142–43). It's so difficult for me to explain that quote from Dr. Campbell, but I understand it from the depths of my very soul. Even my son noticed that my mother seemed to be happy only if I was hurting and was always making jealous comments about me, even in his presence. How very sick that is! It's actually quite disgusting, and I still struggle accepting that it's my reality. She really doesn't love me at all, which is astounding to me.

As teenagers my brother and I became accustomed to being keenly aware of Mom's moods so we could measure each situation and prepare ourselves and others as best we could. We were constantly reading her signals, trying to predict what she would say or do next, and fine-tuning our skills at staying one step ahead of her moods. Adult children like us "may not remember the details of previous attacks but are extremely sensitized to imminent attacks. They remember changes in her tone of voice, her facial expression, and her body language" (Lawson 2000, 135). When Mom was lashing out, severely bummed out, or just being robotic and stoic, we called it "wigging out." We talked in code to let each other know what Mom's state of mind was, and then we walked on eggshells to keep the peace. Even as adults, "we are so afraid of getting in trouble that it becomes easier for us to let her have her way. Even the adult children of a toxic mother still walk on eggshells around her. The fear of her tantrum just isn't worth challenging her in any way" (Campbell 2019, 49).

As I mentioned, my own inclination was to keep the peace as much as possible and do whatever small things I could do to help, like always make my bed, wake everyone up each morning, do the family laundry, and hand-wash her pantyhose each evening when she returned home from work. Things felt so out of control, and those small tasks allowed me to feel some sort of success each day, but I don't remember her ever thanking me or even just acknowledging my efforts. Maybe those were things she expected me to do anyway, or maybe she was so focused on her own pain that she never even noticed. As adults, my brother and I still tend to seek harmony in all situations, probably at an abnormal level, and I know we avoid conflict more than most people because it hits too close to home and brings back the hurt and fear we both experienced.

I have a fairy-tale version of what I wish my mom could be, my "mother imagined," but of course that's not who she was, is or will ever be, which hurts way down deep to the core. She did provide for my brother and me in childhood, and we did have some happy times with her. Once we moved to North Carolina, however, out of every ten experiences with my mom, eight would be extremely difficult, so the two that were good only caused us more pain in the end. Those rare times when she was close to "normal" and not so hard to deal with were extremely deceptive because they led us to think that perhaps she was finally getting better, which of course was never the case. This vicious cycle is what Dr. Sherrie Campbell calls "hoovering" because it sucks you back into the crazy before you even realize it. As she goes on to describe here, "Because of our parents' well-orchestrated moments of intermittent kindness, we get confused. We appear to see they have 'good' in them, but we must come to see that this is just a facade" (2019, 105). I feel like I've been on a scary roller coaster against my will for much of my life, and my therapist has helped me realize that I no longer have to ride that roller coaster.

The realization that I wanted off of this roller coaster and out of this insanity was very hard because I was about to experience a final loss, almost like a death, except my mother was still living. I honestly believe it would be easier if she were no longer here. One last lashing out, or "turn" as Christine Lawson describes it, occurred April 14, 2022, and I haven't seen her or talked to her since that day. My "mother imagined," as I like to call her, is a fictitious character whom I would love to meet some day. Until recently she was someone I thought was real, and I kept waiting for her to reveal herself, but that day would never come.

Poems written by me:

Mother

Nov. 6, 2006

I am done with you
And ready to put you in a box
In the far corners of my mind…
I am totally exhausted
From waiting for you
And wondering what's wrong
And asking myself why…

Glimpses of Love
Feb. 29, 2008

I remember being loved by my mother as a child,
And even into upper elementary school.

But after that she either stopped loving me,
Or just lost the ability to show me any love.

Either way I have experienced loss and abandonment,
And a sadness so deep there are no words to describe it.

My mother has not died, but she left me a long time ago.
Of this I am now certain.

Untitled (about Mom)

Oct. 8, 2008

Like a ball of lead in the gut
It hits me again…
And the familiar fog
Descends upon me
Like a heavy blanket
Weighing me down
Despite all my best efforts.

I don't know what to feel
Or what to do…
Numbness is setting in
After years of constant punishment.

CHAPTER TWO

My Childhood Years

My parents are both from the same small town in southwest Georgia. They attended the same public school, but Dad was five years older and had graduated high school (Class of 1959) by the time my mom started her freshman year (Class of 1964). Mom had two younger siblings and grew up in town, and Dad was the third born of six kids and grew up out in the country on his dad's peanut farm. They married in their hometown in September of 1967 when she was twenty-one and Dad was twenty-six. Seventeen months later, in 1969, they had me, and my brother arrived in 1972 right after my third birthday. Although I believe my mom and dad began to struggle at this time, Mom was a good stay-at-home mother for my brother and me during our early childhood years.

In the years before I started school, we lived in Tampa, Florida, because Dad had taken a job there working for Southern Bell. My mom provided healthy and delicious home-cooked meals daily and even won a few local awards for her cooking. Based on my memories of those years, she kept the house clean and organized, while also meeting our needs. Birthdays and holidays were always celebrated with a special cake and dinner, which was to our delight. My brother and I had all the things we needed for a stable and happy childhood: stories and prayers at bedtime, playing outside, going on walks, riding our bikes, trips to local museums, regular checkups at the doctor and dentist, parental involvement at school, love and support from Mom, and love from Dad, although he was at work most of the time. I don't recall anything lacking from my life during that time. Maybe this is when my "mother imagined" concept was born?

FAMILY PHOTO, SPRING 1972, TAMPA, FLORIDA

What I learned from my mom years later, however, painted a very different picture of how things actually were. Even early in their marriage, she had become very unhappy. When I was five and my brother was two, Dad lost his job with Southern Bell and didn't tell my mother, based on what she shared with me when I was a teenager. She told me that he continued to leave the house dressed for work each day but wasn't actually going to work. Mom assumed he was out looking for another job during this time but will actually never know, nor did my dad ever tell her. My dad probably never knew that she told me about it, so of course I never asked him what happened. Mom said they couldn't pay the bills, and the bank foreclosed on their house in Tampa, so they had to move with two young children. She had loved living in Florida and was so angry that Dad had not been honest with her, causing this major life disruption and stress on their marriage. She still holds intense anger and resentment toward my dad about this time in her life, as well as many other unfortunate events she believed were his fault.

My parents then moved to a small rental house in Marietta, Georgia, and my dad started a new job with Gold Kist, Inc. Their house in Florida would be the first and last house for which they would ever have a mortgage because they could only rent or lease after the foreclosure. After just over a year in Marietta, Dad's job would transfer him to Durham, North Carolina, which meant that we had to find a place to live near his new job. I remember my dad traveling to find a suitable place for us to rent, and I believe my mom deeply resented him for making the decision of where we would live without seeking her input. I think she felt trapped by having to stay in Georgia with two young kids. Even so, Dad found us a two-story townhouse in Cary, which would end up being our home for several years until Dad moved out in December of 1982. My mom, my brother, and I would continue to live there until the fall of 1985, when my mother remarried.

To prepare us for the move in 1976, Dad enticed my brother and me with tales of snow in North Carolina, which made us so excited because we had never seen snow before! Dad's charisma and excitement about the move made us feel happy about it, but Mom was not at all happy about our impending move. I remember her crying a lot and worrying specifically about her beautiful ferns that wouldn't like the Carolina winters. She was very stressed and unhappy, and now that I look back on that time, perhaps it was the beginning of the end for her marriage with my dad.

We moved to North Carolina in late October of 1976, and I remember starting second grade on Halloween because at that time kids could still wear costumes to school to celebrate the holiday. I was so excited to wear my witch costume, which had always been my favorite! It was handmade by my mom, and the pointy hat had silver rickrack around the edge, which I loved. That costume still hangs in my closet to this very day and is very special because it is something that my mother made just for me.

IT SNOWED IN JANUARY OF 1977.

MY BROTHER AND I WERE DELICHTED!

My brother was in prekindergarten (pre-K) at the time, and Mom got a job as a pre-K teacher at the church that offered the program where he was enrolled. She seemed to enjoy her time there, although I learned from her years later that she had settled on that job since there were no available teaching jobs in the local public school system at that time. Apparently she had hoped for a job teaching vocational education at the high school or community college level, but there were no such opportunities then. It was during this time that she met two ladies who would end up being close friends of hers, Jerry and Marta, although I don't think she has heard from them in many years. My mother has very few close friends.

Much to my delight, Mom enrolled me in dance lessons soon after we moved to North Carolina, and dance became an obsession of mine until high school graduation in 1987. I am thankful for the opportunity to learn ballet, tap, and jazz, and I acknowledge both of my parents in this effort because Mom was always there to take me to class and pick me up, and Dad was paying for my lessons. I remember Dad picking me up only one time, and he took me to Burger King that night for my favorite classic chicken sandwich, which I devoured in just a few bites after working so hard in dance class! It's funny how I remember that particular evening so vividly and with such simple happiness. My brother enjoyed tee ball, and Mom signed him up to be on a team. His interest would later turn to tennis once he was in high school, and he even lettered in the sport. He and Dad used to play tennis at the local courts near where we lived, which helped to fine tune my brother's tennis skills.

Our black poodle, Jocko, was Mom's pride and joy, and it was apparent to us that she loved him more than most people, and maybe more than she loved us. My brother would often taunt Jocko, as little boys sometimes do. Jocko would growl at him and bare his teeth, which would immediately elicit a sharp reprimand from my mother. Of course my brother thought it was funny most of the time, then Jocko actually bit a few of his friends, one of whom sustained a severe wound that required stitches, and my dad reacted by taking him away to be put to sleep. My mother begged my father not to take Jocko away; she was very upset, and I remember how terrible that time was. She was inconsolable and so enraged at my dad, which only added to the layers of anger she already felt toward him. We never saw Jocko again, and I don't recall us ever discussing what happened to him. I felt so sorry for my mom, and I felt helpless because I couldn't do anything to improve the situation.

PICTURE OF ME (IN DANCE COSTUME) WITH JOCKO, 1982

My memories of home during these elementary school years in North Carolina are dominated by my mom's stress and unhappiness, and my dad was almost always away at work, so most of the parenting duties fell on her. Mom would often stay in their bedroom for hours on end talking on the phone to her sister, my sweet Aunt Jane, and lamenting how very unhappy she was. I later learned that Aunt Jane and her husband sent money to Mom a few times, although I don't know the details of how that came to pass. My grandmother had also sent money to my mom, but I didn't learn that until I was well into adulthood and found letters Mom had written thanking my grandmother for the financial gifts. There may be other family members who sent her money as well, but I'll likely never know. I don't doubt that my mother struggled financially, but it pains me to know that relatives sent her money, then she would criticize them openly, even when my brother and I could hear.

I cried a lot when I was in elementary school, and for years I thought that was just how I handled fatigue and stress. My tears would often come after dance class when I was just exhausted, or when my mother was trying to help me with homework that I didn't understand, which always resulted in her yelling at me and biting her tongue at me in anger. Now, however, I believe many of my tears were a symptom of the tension I so often felt around my mother but couldn't recognize or verbalize at my young age. I'm sure I was internalizing her stress because I couldn't figure out how to help her or how to make things better, nor did I really grasp what was going on. To me that was normal.

CHAPTER THREE

My Teenage and College Years

I wrote poems starting in late elementary school, and I also kept journals where I wrote down some of the most painful times. These pieces of my personal history are treasures to me, and I never once considered not keeping them. To me they are like windows to my soul, and they remain carefully preserved in a container inside my closet. Now that I am a middle-aged adult, re-reading what I wrote over the years has been eye opening and has forced me to remember some things I had forgotten. Many of my poems have a sweet and happy tone because I've always had a deep optimism in my heart, but some of them are so sad because they describe the pain I often felt. Likewise, many of my journal entries describe my immense sadness, anger, and confusion over my mom's behavior toward me, and these entries span over forty years. I'm often amazed when I read entries that were written decades apart yet describe the same erratic behavior from my mother and my own familiar pain.

When I was in junior high (August 1981–June 1984), I remember vividly how often I felt like I just wanted to die. I was never suicidal and was far too scared to try anything anyway, but I wanted God to reach down, pluck me from the earth, and just take me away. My therapist explained to me that this desire to die without actually wanting to commit suicide is called "suicidal ideation," and I was glad it actually had a name. Truly I did not want to kill myself, but I very much wanted to disappear or just evaporate.

MY BROTHER AND I, 1985

Those years were so depressing, as I know they are for many adolescents, including those lucky enough to have stable family situations, but I think that time was significantly harder for me. Although I often wanted to just disappear, if God Himself had given me that option, I could never have left my brother behind to deal with the craziness on his own. As his big sister, I felt fiercely protective over him, and I still do on some level, although of course it's different since we are both adults in middle age. At my insistence, he and I made a promise when we were just kids never to part without saying "I love you."

I remember everything being so difficult during that time, like a heavy weight was on my shoulders, and I couldn't get it off. Sometimes it was as if my lungs were too heavy for me to breathe. I was intensely aware of my parents' unhappiness and even asked my mom several months earlier if they were going to get divorced. Well, it wasn't too long before they sat my brother and me down to let us know they were separating, and Dad moved out right before Christmas of my eighth-grade year (December 10, 1982). Even though my brother and I weren't used to spending that much time with him, it was still a big adjustment for us. Dad had always spent a lot of time at work, likely escaping the stress and unhappiness at home, but before he and Mom separated, at least we had him home in the late evenings and on weekends. At this point Mom was stressed out, angry, and sad all of the time. She was taking paralegal classes at night and had started working at a local law firm, which had to have been very challenging. I found myself constantly try-ing to cheer her up and justify her behaviors to myself and others as natural reactions to these recent life stresses. The inherent codependency is so obvious to me now.

During this time I cried a lot and rarely felt happy, which I realize isn't atypical for an adolescent female, but I believe it occurred far more often for me. Looking back, I realize it was probably sheer exhaustion from trying to fig-ure out what was wrong with my mom and why I couldn't make her happy. Just as it was when I was in elementa-ry school, I could never lessen her stress level, and I didn't understand why it never got better, although at the time I wasn't aware of the real issues at play. In one of my journals from that time, I found a quote from Homer in a poetry book that really resonated with me: "The lot of man is to suffer and die." I look back now and feel deep sympathy for my younger self that I took note of such a depressing quote and wrote it down in my journal.

One afternoon in eighth grade, I was waiting for Mom to pick me up from school, and she had not arrived yet. I have vivid memories of this afternoon because it really scared me, which may sound silly, but it's true. I waited for what felt like a very long time, and I watched as teachers and other staff had long since driven off. I don't recall how much time had actually passed, but I think she was about two hours late, and I was beginning to worry. We didn't have cell phones at the time, so my only option would have been to try to get back into the school office to call home, but she showed up before I had to resort to that. I remember her pulling up with this big smile on her face and looking so very happy, while I had been worried and scared, which was odd to me. She did not acknowledge how late she was or how I was feeling at that point. When I got in the front seat of her 1972 Chevy Caprice Classic, she had a large fabric purse with a small puppy inside it. Indeed, this puppy was terribly cute, but I realized at that moment that he was more important than I was. She said she had seen her electrolysis lady, who had shown her some puppies that afternoon, and of course the rest was history. The new puppy was named "Buster" and became the main focus of her life. "Buster" ended up biting me on the face twice, and one of those bites required a trip to the emergency room. He also chewed on my new Bass sandals, rendering one of them useless, and I remember feeling so devastated. My mother didn't buy me a new pair to replace them, even knowing how long I had saved my own money to buy them. On all three of those instances, she blamed me and defended him of course.

On another occasion during that same school year, my mom was frantically trying to gather her things and get to class in Durham, where she was studying to be a paralegal by taking night classes. I realize she was under immense stress at this time because she and my dad were separated, and she was dealing with additional challenges. Entering the workforce after years of staying at home with us was already upon her, and I can only imagine how scary that was. On this particular night, I was sitting on the living room floor with my back against the wall just under the main front window, and I had my knees pulled up so that I was sitting in a tight ball. I was crying my eyes out and felt so down, but I don't remember if there was anything in particular that had upset me, or if I was just feeling awful that evening. My mom stopped in the hallway, looked at me with disgust, and said angrily, "Are you going to be all right?!" I replied yes but was still crying of course, so she then replied, "You aren't going to do anything stupid, are you?" I replied with "Of course not," then she headed on to class while I was still there on the floor upset. I have no memory of where my brother was that night.

I remember feeling so low that I honestly wanted to die. As I mentioned at the beginning of this chapter, I was experiencing "suicidal ideation" and was likely very depressed at that time. Now that I'm a parent, I simply cannot imagine leaving my son upset and alone at home like she left me on that night. My "mother imagined" would have put down her things that instant and held me until I stopped crying. She would have asked me what was wrong and guided me through some possible solutions. She would not have gone to class that night and instead would have made me her priority.

My parents' divorce was final in July of 1984, right before I started tenth grade. Mom had begun dating an older man whose daughter worked in the same office building as she did. He was a widower and a retired textile engineer whose house wasn't even three miles from our townhouse. My brother and I liked him, and he treated us with love and kindness, always being gracious to our father when he was in town to see us. They got married in October of 1985, when I was in the eleventh grade, so we moved into his house right behind my high school. He was twenty-one years her senior, and he opened his heart and home to us without hesitation. My brother and I each had our own rooms just as before when we lived in our townhouse, and our stepdad loved us as his own. He often showed us small acts of kindness, like warming cheese bread sticks in the oven for us so we could enjoy them before leaving for school.

One time when I was in high school, my brother and I were standing in the hallway, and Mom was sitting in her bed sobbing heavily, which was painful to witness. I don't know where our stepdad was at that moment, but he may have been at choir practice (he had an amazing tenor voice) or watching a football game on TV with his best friend across town. Obviously Mom was very upset, so we asked her what was wrong, to which she replied, "I want to blow my f-ing brains out!" I remember feeling that familiar heavy weight in the pit of my stomach and not knowing how to respond, just standing there feeling numb and shell shocked by what she had just said with such anger. Right after that she said something about wishing she had never had children because they were "life sentences." I don't remember what my brother and I said or did after that, which is weird to me. I assume that we just walked away, but I simply can't recall; it's like I went blank after that. Such an experience leaves teenage kids feeling so helpless and worthless, not to mention afraid. I don't remember my brother and me ever discussing it later; most likely we just moved on like we always did.

On another occasion Mom threw the photo album of her 1967 wedding to my father in the grill on the upstairs deck and burned it. I remember feeling so shocked and upset because that was a piece of history from my parents that I would never see again, nor could I ever share it with my own family one day. She seemed brazen and proud of herself, apparently even enjoying the spectacle of it all. I realize now that it was probably helpful to her if she was trying to deal with anger toward my dad, but she should have handled it differently since my brother and I were at home to witness the scene. I really think that experience was more upsetting to me than I ever allowed myself to admit.

Around that same time, one of my best friends and I were regulars at a teen nightclub in Raleigh, and it was there that I met Terry, the young man who would be my husband. It was my senior year of high school on the night before my eighteenth birthday, and we found ourselves at our favorite spot for pizza, Diet Coke, and dancing! When the DJ changed the dance music to a slow and sultry Freddy Jackson song, my friend and I walked off the dance floor to take a quick break, and three guys walked closely by us. Terry took my arm and asked me to dance, and one of his friends did the same to my friend, while the third guy just waited out this slow dance off of the dance floor. I had danced many times with some arbitrary guy that had also been in attendance at our teen hang out, but I never let a single one kiss me, nor did I give any of them my number. Well, soon after our slow dance started, Terry actually kissed me! My friend was slow dancing near us, and she was nearly undone by this shocking occurrence! Each time we turned to face each other, she made faces at me that the guys couldn't see because she knew that I never kissed the guys with whom I danced. When we left that night, I told her I was "gonna marry that boy," but I didn't even know his last name. I had given him my phone number, though, which was a first for me.

Terry and I fell in love that spring, and I invited him to my senior prom in May. When I graduated high school in June of 1987, he was there in attendance with my family, which was wonderful for me. Mom then treated us to a weekend trip to Myrtle Beach to celebrate, which was a delightful surprise, and Terry was my invited guest. It was that weekend when I first said "I love you" to him, and he reciprocated.

During the first few months of our new relationship, I had to explain my mother to him, which of course was always a significant challenge. The best I could do at the time was to tell him that she's "been through a lot in her life" and that she could be "hard to deal with." It was always so difficult to explain Mom to others, and I found myself wishing for a more concrete response, like "My mom passed away a few years ago," or "My mom has a mental illness and sometimes has erratic behavior." Either of those would have immediately explained to other people that her behavior doesn't fall in the normal realm, but those were never options for me. I really needed to label the situation with something tangible and specific so folks could begin to understand. It would be decades later when I finally realized the word "toxic" best described my relationship with my mother, and I also took the first steps to come to terms with the fact that my "mother imagined" was merely a fantasy.

MY SENIOR PROM, MAY 1987

Since Terry is two years older than I, we were both in college at the same time and dated all throughout our college years. We spent most weekends together at his dad's house and soaked in every minute we were together. There were times when we went to my mom and stepdad's house, too, and they both loved Terry. In fact, Mom seemed to like Terry much more than she liked me, but that was fine with me because that meant she was happy if I wanted him to come over. One time there was a snowstorm expected, and Mom told me it was fine to ask Terry to come over and get snowed in with us, which delighted me to no end. We did just that and had a ball! My brother was in high school at the time, and he liked Terry too.

During our first year of dating, we were leaving his dad's house one evening, likely headed to a local dance club that we loved, and something had happened with my mom, although I don't remember the details, which is not atypical. Even early on in our relationship, Terry was grasping the intensity of the situation and told me that one day my mom would find herself all alone, and it would be completely her own fault. At the time it was so hard for me to hear him say that, but honestly, I couldn't have disagreed with him because I knew deep down inside that it was true. That night was nearly forty years ago, and my mother has pushed away nearly all of her family members and friends, so undoubtedly, Terry's prediction has come to pass.

As Stephanie Foo puts it, "I probably hated my mother for being impossible to please. But I also loved her, and so

I guess I must have felt guilty, too, and frightened" (2022, 13). I can honestly say that I don't love my mother anymore. I also know deep down inside that she doesn't love me and hasn't for a long time. That may be hard for others to understand, and it's hard for me to put it down on paper, but it's simply the honest truth. The part of me that once loved her and kept trying to win her love and approval has been beaten to a pulp by her constant criticism and hateful argumentative responses over every little thing without exception. There is no turning back from here.

Poem written by me:

Untitled (about Mom)
Sept. 18, 1989

I was twenty years old and a junior in college when I wrote this.

She has loved me; she has hated me.
She has cared for me during the hardest times of my life.

She has comforted me; she has given so much to me.
But she has caused great pain and frustration in my life.

She has bragged about me; she has been by my side.
She has also made me wish I had never been born.

She does not tell me she's proud of me.
She's never told me I'm pretty. To her, I'm just mediocre.

She has made me feel like I'm not good enough.
She has told me that I will make the same mistakes she's made.
I feel such love and hope in life until I'm in her presence…

She makes me feel like I must be defensive.
I don't share with her my dreams for the future.

Sometimes I really wonder if she truly loves me.
She is no longer the one that I go to for love and support.
I must find strength from other sources in my life.

CHAPTER FOUR

My Wedding

Up front I must admit that this is an extremely difficult topic for me. I doubt I have the emotional bandwidth to even briefly describe this painful experience, let alone write it in a way that comes close to explaining the wrath of my mother. My husband and I went through so many difficult challenges with her as we planned our 1993 wedding, and we both harbor intense emotions attached to this occasion that will be embedded in our psyches for as long as we have a working memory.

On the actual day of our wedding, my mother never even spoke to me. She did not hug me or interact with me in any way, only standing near me for a few required wedding photos of the family with the bride. Even then she didn't touch me, not even to put her arm around me for the mother-daughter prewedding photograph. It was so painful and unnatural that it's still hard to believe even more than thirty years later. Oh, how I wanted her to be a loving mom on that day by some miracle, and at last be my "mother imagined," but it was not to be.

THIS WEDDING-DAY PHOTO IS STILL HARD TO LOOK AT.

IT WAS EXTREMELY TENSE AND UNCOMFORTABLE.

As Sherrie Campbell so adequately explains in her poignant book, "With toxic mothers, there is no such thing as enough. They will do just about anything to spoil any occasion where someone else is the center of attention, particularly the child they have cast as the scapegoat" (2019, 47). When I read this quote, it feels like a knife in my chest and a heavy lead ball in my gut because it's so painfully true about my own experience as we prepared for and experienced our wedding. It's sad that such a meaningful and life-changing event conjures up so many awful memories, but that's the usual pattern when it comes to dealing with my mom.

My husband proposed to me on Christmas Eve of 1991 when I was twenty-two and he was twenty-four, and we set a date in late June of 1993, which provided us a long engagement. He was in his final year of college in 1991–92, then in the 1992–93 school year, we were both teaching middle school, so it made sense that we would marry in June of 1993 when school was out for summer vacation. Right away we experienced antagonistic reactions from my mother, even with the first decision of where to get married. She of course wanted us to get married at her church, but we were both members at Terry's home church, which was obviously our choice for our special event.

My mom made every decision, no matter how minute or seemingly insignificant, into a huge challenge that usually led to her getting her way because we didn't have the emotional energy to fight the battle any longer. At one point she even suggested that my dad not be seated with the family up front during our ceremony, which was appalling to me. Our wedding director handled that situation by citing etiquette rules and my wishes as his daughter, much to our relief.

This excerpt from my journal on August 22, 1992, helps me remember:

Dad is in town and staying at my house. He and I had a long talk about getting me down the aisle. Brad and Dad will share the job. Details later.

What I had really wanted deep down in my gut was for my brother to give me away by himself, not my brother and my dad as I had discussed with them earlier and written in my journal, nor my dad or stepdad individually. My wish would not come true, however, because in January of 1993 my brother enlisted in the United States Army and would likely not be able to attend my wedding at all, which left me deciding between my dad and my stepdad. Since my mother loathed my father, and she and my stepfather were funding our wedding, I felt like I should acquiesce when my mom expressed her wish that my stepdad be the one to walk me down the aisle. She pointed out that my dad wasn't paying a dime for anything, which was true as far as I knew. Of course that put me between a rock and a hard place and made me feel guilty about not involving my dad. I felt so trapped.

Months before our wedding, I wrote my dad a heartfelt note, and I did the same to my paternal grandmother, who I knew would not understand why my dad wasn't walking me down the aisle. Gosh, that was so incredibly difficult for me, and I kept copies of those letters. At the ceremony my dad was all smiles and held his head high, though, which made me feel so thankful. To his credit, he never lashed out at me or made me feel bad about my decision. Had the tables been turned, my mother would have been hell on wheels to say the least. She would never have handled herself as well as my father did, which is so ironic to me. In the end it turned out fine when my stepdad walked me down the aisle, and my dad handled himself with grace and dignity, not once aiming any anger in my direction.

Interestingly enough, my mom and stepdad ended up flying my brother in to attend my wedding as a surprise, and to my sheer delight, he was waiting for me in my dressing room at the church when I arrived on my wedding day! This was a lovely and thoughtful wedding gift to me, but had I known that my brother would be coming, he could have escorted me down the aisle just like I wanted. My mom probably realized that and thus didn't let me know, all the while justifying it to herself because it was a "surprise" for me. I'm certain that she wanted my dad's family to see my stepdad walking me down the aisle. I know that must have been really hard on my father.

MY SWEET STEPDAD AND I ABOUT TO WALK DOWN THE AISLE

Another excerpt from my journal reminds me of how hard it was with my mom, February 9, 1993:

Mom has "lost it" again. I feel so confused. I can never, ever please her, yet she won't tell me what she wants. Every time we "talk" on the phone, she tells me how stupid, stubborn, and self-centered I am. She is out of control.

I don't know why she says those things to me—I do not know what the hell it is that I do to her. You'd think she had not one drop of love for me. I wonder what it is I feel for her.

She tears me down, bit by bit, as painfully as possible. She does not have the ability to step outside of herself and really listen to what she says to people. She tells me off, she tells Bill off, she tells Ebie off, and she runs down everyone she knows.

I wish she could never reach me and say all of those cruel things to me. She loves to see me hurt—like she does. She is ruining the planning for our wedding, and she is not happy for us.

About two weeks prior to our June 26 wedding, I had gone to my mother's house (twenty miles away) to see our wedding presents that were arriving, mainly from family in Georgia. In those days the traditional gifts were china, crystal, and silver, all of which we were receiving on a regular basis by that point. Mom had set up tables draped in white tablecloths with tulle accents in my old bedroom, and all of the presents that had arrived were displayed beautifully. I remember commenting that I wish I could see our gifts as they arrived, but I was just making conversation and enjoying the excitement of it all. Truly I was not implying that I wanted to take them from their display at her house and keep them at my house instead.

Well, my mother was obviously offended by my statement because on June 15, she and my stepdad brought all of our wedding presents to my little rental house when I was not home. They just left them all on the side porch without a note or a phone call to let me know. When I arrived home, I literally felt sick when I saw the piles of presents they had left. Their actions felt so deceptive and underhanded. Terry and my future father-in-law came over right away to help me get the gifts into the house and also to console me. What my mother and stepdad did made me feel terrible, and again there was no explanation or discussion about it that day or later. Now I realize it was another one of my mother's tantrums in reaction to my comment about not being able to see our wedding presents as they arrived, and she had enlisted the help of my stepfather, who always complied to keep the peace.

There were several bridal showers in the months leading up to our June wedding, and my mom attended most of the ones to which she was invited. I was greatly relieved that she behaved fairly well, likely because there were colleagues and friends in attendance. She is quite capable of being very polished and professional when situations require it. When it came time for my bridesmaid's brunch a week before the wedding, however, my mother was not there. My maid of honor and her mother hosted the event, and it was held at a local tea room, where everything looked so pretty. My heart sank when my mother never showed up, and I was embarrassed and deeply hurt. I felt certain she would attend, just as she had previous bridal showers, but that was not to be. She and I never once discussed it, so I still don't know why she didn't come, not that it would matter at this point. Like all other negative situations involving my mom, there was never any discussion, apology, attempts at understanding, or resolution.

My mom spent over eight hundred hours stitching a traditional wedding sampler for us and presented it as her special gift to us on the evening of our rehearsal dinner. It's so very beautiful and should bring us joy, but sadly it represents such a difficult and terrible time in our lives that it's no longer hanging up in our house. Instead, it now sits alongside other special items in the guest room closet because looking at it only conjures up painful memories. Creating this wedding sampler for us was such a lovely gesture from the mother of the bride, which again makes me feel at odds with myself and with my memories of our wedding. How in the world could my mother treat us the way she did yet put so much time into such a meaningful and personalized gift? Maybe she was seeking the admiration from attendees by presenting such a gift to us? I can't make any sense of it, and I guess I will never know.

Finally, the big day arrived. As is customary in a traditional wedding, the mother of the bride will stand just before the bride's entrance into the church, thereby signaling the congregation to also stand in honor of the bridal procession.

It's a beautiful etiquette ritual because everyone stands for the bride to make her grand appearance. When it was time for me to walk down the aisle on my stepdad's arm, my mother did stand in customary practice, but when she turned to look in my direction, her expression was forced and robotic, completely without feeling. She glared at me with a look of total disdain, as if she truly hated even being there. She wasn't the proud and loving mother overflowing with emotion at her daughter's marriage ceremony, my "mother imagined," whom I so desperately wanted. Her expression was so cold and hateful that I couldn't believe it, and I was crestfallen, as I'd been so many times before. Since this was the biggest day of my life thus far, I had hoped she would soften and actually experience some level of joy, but I was again mistaken. Her face showed no kindness or love on any level toward me, as if I had committed some heinous crime against her, which was so baffling to me. I was about to walk down the aisle at my wedding, though, so I pushed those thoughts to the far recesses of my brain and immediately focused on the task at hand, never making eye contact with her again. I reminded myself that those in attendance had come because of their love for Terry and me, and their purpose was to witness and share this beautiful event with us. Focusing on that would help me cope.

Once we were at the altar together and the service was in progress, the time came to say our wedding vows. When it was Terry's turn, he took one look at me and broke down in tears, unable to speak for a few moments. I knew this wasn't just because of our special moment and the love we shared. His sudden tears came because he knew what we had both been through over the past eighteen months of planning. He knew what my mother had put me through especially, and it was more than he could bear. Everyone saw it as a tender and loving moment, which of course it was, but I knew in the core of my soul that it had been prompted by my mother's wrath.

TERRY AND I ON OUR WEDDING DAY

There were just over three hundred attendees at our wedding since we obliged my mother by inviting everyone she suggested, so it was bigger than what we had originally planned. I had several relatives from southwest Georgia who made the six-hundred-mile trip just to be there for us, which meant more to me than they will ever know. Terry had lots of local family members who were there, of course, and we both had many friends in attendance for our special day. In the end, it was still the most special day of our lives because it was the day we married each other. I just couldn't believe that my own mother had not so much as given me a hug on that day. She said nothing to me at all and never even smiled at me; she did not speak to my husband either. It was truly unbelievable. I understand the typical family stress and drama that comes along with a wedding, and I recognize the mother-daughter tension that happens so often as well. Still, I just can't reconcile her behavior toward us, and more specifically me, over the months of planning for our special event, as well as on the actual day itself. In no way did she act like a mother, and certainly not my "mother imagined." It was as if she truly wanted to rob us of our joy and happiness.

My dad gave us eight hundred dollars cash to use on our honeymoon, which was just a simple trip to Sunset Beach, North Carolina. He also gave us a really nice set of stainless-steel pots and pans that we used for thirty years and are keeping for our son's first apartment.

A few weeks after our wedding, my mother mailed us a hard copy of the entire multipage invoice for our reception.

She and my stepdad had paid for it, which of course we acknowledged and appreciated, but she wanted to make sure we knew how much it had cost them. I had to remind myself that our reception was what my mother wanted and in fact had insisted upon; it wasn't what we had originally planned or expected. She wanted things done her way, likely to make her look good for the invited guests, which included her family and my dad's, and that's what it boiled down to.

My mother never reached out to check on us as we were experiencing our new life together, not even a phone call or note in the mail. In fact, we didn't hear from her for a long time after our wedding. It was as if we had done something horrible to her, which is astounding to me. What in the world was wrong anyway? It's not like we had experienced some major blow up with her, and truly we had done everything possible to pacify my mother during our wedding planning. I realize there is no answer to that question; it was just my mother reacting to everything in her usual way, spreading anger everywhere and leaving family and friends to wonder why she was behaving in such a negative way. My "mother imagined" would have checked in after our honeymoon just to say hello and find out how we were. She would have enjoyed viewing our wedding pictures and reminiscing about our big day, but of course that didn't happen. My sweet stepfather didn't check in on us either, and I am certain that was because he was always pacifying my mom to keep the peace and prevent additional meltdowns. The proof album sent to my mother from our wedding photographer was returned to him unopened, so she chose not to even view our wedding pictures, which was so painful.

CHAPTER FIVE

My Early Career Years

When I graduated college with my undergraduate degree in 1991, I took advantage of a program at a Nissan dealership in Raleigh and bought my very first car all on my own. The program allowed a recent college graduate who had landed her first job to buy a car with no money down and no payment for three months, which was perfect for me. My parents didn't give me a car in high school, and since my only job during my teen years was babysitting, I didn't have the means to save up for one. Well, to say that I was over-the-moon excited about this opportunity was an understatement! Terry went with me, and we had researched how things would happen and what I should insist upon as I bought my first car. When we drove off the lot that day, I was overjoyed and so proud of myself, and of course I couldn't wait to show my mom. My "mother imagined" was going to be so excited for me and acknowledge this major life milestone with me, but that was not what happened. I pulled into the driveway at my mom and stepdad's house, and we anxiously waited for my mother to return home from work. When she finally arrived, she parked on the side of the street since my car was in her driveway, then proceeded to walk right by Terry and me as we stood beside my brand-new Nissan without saying a word. What a deflating moment that was.

It occurs to me now that I'm in my middle-age years that my mother really struggled when others experienced good things in life, even if those people were her own children. For some reason, it was especially problematic for her when I experienced success and happiness. She could never be happy for me or share joy with me, nor was she usually happy for my brother either, unless of course other folks were there to witness her reactions. As my son pointed out to me when he was in middle school, she actually behaves better when I'm down, sick, or hurting. As he often said to me in his early teenage years, "Mom, she likes to see you hurt."

I was a middle and high school Spanish and English-as-a-second-language teacher from 1991 to 2003. I went on to work at the North Carolina Department of Public Instruction from 2003 to 2007, then accepted a position in the largest school district in the state, Wake County Schools, which is where I was educated myself. My first job right after college graduation was in a school district not far from Terry's dad's house, which made me realize that I could probably stay there and not at home. In September of 1991, I moved out of my stepdad's house and stayed in an extra bedroom at my future father-in-law's house, which immediately made a difference in my life. Terry's dad and I would eat dinner together each night, and I felt total peace there at his house. It was a blessing to be there and away from my mother's critical words and severe lows. Terry was in college for one more year because of transferring from community college, so he was away much of the time, and I was busy working.

February of 1996 brought with it a very serious and scary time because my mother attempted suicide by taking a handful of narcotics that had been prescribed to her for pre-menopausal migraines. She also ingested several Dramamine pills, which I assume was to quell the impending nausea and prevent vomiting. I received a phone call from my stepdad in the wee hours of the morning and was completely shocked. Believe it or not, I had never even considered that my mother would do such a thing, but then again, at that time I had not come to terms with the fact that her issues were not just reactions to life's stresses. I would later learn that my mom called her brother in Georgia to tell him about the pills she had taken, almost as if to taunt him, so he was also aware of what was happening, even from six hundred miles away. He told her to tell my stepdad, who immediately called 911, which dispatched an ambulance. My uncle and maternal grandmother hit the road and drove all day to be there with us, and my brother did the same, driving from MacDill Air Force Base in Florida, where he was stationed at the time.

I have memories of this traumatic event in bits and piec-es, but I remember being in a small room with my family and a few doctors, who asked if my mother had been depressed. My uncle was a psychologist, so I felt like his responses held much more weight than mine, but both he and I confirmed that based on our observations of her, she had been depressed for some time. I remember nearly falling out on the floor when they asked this question; at that time I didn't even have the words to explain her many psychological issues. My mom would later express her intense anger at both of us for telling the doctors that she had been depressed, and she continued to bring it back up in conversation for many years to come. When my brother and I were in her hospital room, she was intubated and unable to speak, having been in a coma for over twenty-four hours. She looked furious, and she pointed to a clipboard and red pen, which I handed to her right away. It was then that she angrily scribbled "I want to die" and hurled the clipboard at me like a Frisbee, hitting me in my left arm. At that point my brother and I simply left her room, not really knowing what to do next and still reeling from the insanity of this entire event. I remember the lump in my throat and how awful it all felt.

In my sixth year of teaching (1996–1997), I decided to go to graduate school at my alma mater, Meredith College, in Raleigh. I secured financial aid, worked full time while taking classes toward my MEd degree, and finally defended my thesis in August of 2002. To my surprise and delight, my thesis was awarded the Graduate Thesis Award by my college and was sent on to the University of Georgia at Athens to compete with others that had been selected by their institutions of higher education. When I told my mom about my award, she responded as she always did when I had good news, with a curt obligatory comment that had no sincerity behind it whatsoever: "That's nice," she said in her robotic tone of voice. It was as if she was actually jealous of me, which in fact I now believe to be the case. It didn't make sense to me because my "mother imagined" would never be jealous or envious of me. She would celebrate my successes and be my biggest champion of course.

My mother was always reminding me of the things she could do that I could not, and I never balked at that; in fact, I agreed wholeheartedly with her. She seemed to enjoy pointing out my ineptitude as she emphasized her own strengths and many accomplishments. In her view, she was always better at everything and always worked harder than I did. I wasn't any of the things she was when she was my age, and I never tried to be. She was head cheerleader, was homecoming queen, and won more than one local beauty pageant while in high school. She was also an accomplished swimmer, lifeguard, expert cook, and seamstress, which was impressive. In her high school yearbook, she was chosen for two superlatives her senior year, which says a lot about her involvement and popularity at that time. What's interesting is how often she would bring these things up to me as if we were in some tense competition with each other. I was my own person with different interests and directions in life; I didn't even try to do the same things she had done, yet she seemed to view me as threatening competition. My "mother imagined" would have been proud of me for my own individual (albeit different) accomplishments rather than constantly comparing them to her own, while reminding me that her accomplishments were greater and took more effort.

Toward the end of my years in the classroom (1991–2002), I won "Teacher of the Year" at the high school where I was teaching, and I also won a few small local awards. My mother attended all of the events related to these awards, which was surprising to me at the time. Of course it made me happy that she would support me like that, and I again felt that false sense of love that was always intensely confusing and made me continue to hope for her to get better. Again I realize that perhaps her attendance was due to the fact that others would be watching her. Behind the scenes when it was just the two of us, she was never proud of me, never praised me, and never congratulated me.

In January of 2003, I was hired as a consultant at the North Carolina Department of Public Instruction (NCD-PI) in downtown Raleigh, which was the biggest job opportunity of my life, bar none. At that time my mother was a paralegal and worked for the North Carolina General Assembly, so our buildings were actually parallel to each other on the government "mall," and we both parked in the same parking deck right across the street. Sometimes I would walk over to see her, and she would parade me up and down the halls introducing me proudly to attorneys, lobbyists, and others. She was so bubbly during those times, so again I would cling to the false hope that she might get better and be more like that on a regular basis. Then other times I'd walk over to take her a Diet Coke and a Zero bar (her favorite candy bar), and she'd glare at me like I had two heads and ask me what I was doing over there.

My "mother imagined" would have been thrilled to see me at her office any time and would have given me a big hug and said, "Let's go grab some lunch, honey." Gosh, I can see the whole wonderful scene in my mind like it's actually real! In reality, she was rarely happy to see me and instead treated me like a total nuisance, unless of course her colleagues were nearby, prompting much better behavior. She never initiated lunch or a quick meeting in the parking deck; if those things ever happened, they were always orchestrated by me with much effort, which became so exhausting and meaningless.

CHAPTER SIX

My Son's Arrival

My mother had always told me that a woman's body is at its peak for having babies at age twenty-five. I don't know if that was her opinion on the topic or if it was actually what medicine was telling folks at that time. Maybe she had been telling me this because I was in my mid thirties at this point and was probably not going to have any babies, meaning that she had accomplished something that I could not. She had me at age twenty-two and my brother at age twenty-five, so according to her, she did everything perfectly, by the book, and in line with what the field of obstetrics was saying. Her subtle message to me during many of our conversations was about her superiority. As I mentioned in chapter three, it's interesting to note that numerous times in my young adult life, she referred to children as "life sentences." Did she have any awareness of how that made my brother and me feel? A mother should never say such a thing, especially in front of her own children.

As for me, I was adamant against having kids for as long as I can remember. All I remember thinking was, why in the world would I bring a child into this insanity and dysfunction (meaning the incredibly unstable situation with my mother)? I continued feeling that way through college and most of my twenties until Terry and I realized we should think long and hard about parenthood before our biological clocks left us behind. In 1997 when I was twenty-eight and he was thirty, we stopped preventing pregnancy and thought we'd let nature take its course.

Well, things didn't happen as we had hoped, so several months later we had some infertility testing, and Terry had surgery, none of which seemed to make a difference. Six years later, in December of 2004, when we were at my dear friend's graduation for her master's degree, her mother (a retired nurse) looked me up and down, then told me emphatically that I was pregnant. I playfully replied with a chuckle saying she was crazy, but I knew I had already missed two periods and realized it could actually be possible. I had taken so many pregnancy tests a few years back that I didn't even want to try that again. My friend's mother said that if I didn't take a pregnancy test the very next morning, she would go to my house in person and make me take one in her presence.

I did as I was told and took that pregnancy test, and lo and behold, it was positive! wow! To say that we were in shock is a severe understatement. Of course I started a brand-new journal, and we started sharing our news since I was already almost three months along. We told our closest friends, Terry's mom, my dad, and my brother first, but we waited awhile to tell my mom and stepdad. We decided on a cute card that had baby feet on the front, and we delivered it to them in person in January of 2005. My stepdad was always cautious around my mother for obvious reasons, but he was happy for us as we expected. Mom behaved for the most part, but her reaction was cold and robotic; it was not the reaction my "mother imagined" would have had. Of course my Pollyanna imagination had pictured her giving each of us a big hug with genuine joy and congratulations—an outpouring of love to share in our special announcement. I actually can't believe that I was still expecting her to show joy; wasn't I an expert by this time in predicting her reactions? I'm astounded and disgusted with myself at how I kept hoping for something different, even after everything I'd been through with her.

I was estranged from my mother most of the time from 2003 through 2005, so even though I saw her in January when my husband and I shared our exciting news in person, my second and third trimesters came when we weren't communicating, which made the situation even more sad. Mom never asked about any of my baby showers or expressed an interest in attending, and as I look back through my journals and scrapbooks where I kept detailed notes, I don't think we even included her on the invitation lists for obvious reasons. A close friend remembers me saying that my mother was actually going to attend one of the showers, though, so it's possible that I sent her an invitation if she had mentioned wanting to go, but I really don't remember. What I do know, as my close friends have reminded me, is that she wasn't in attendance at any of our baby showers. This was yet another time when she struggled to be happy for us, even though she already knew that our son would be her only grandchild since my brother was not having kids. I desperately wanted a mother with whom I could share this joyful time in my life, and who could offer me her advice and tell me it would be all right, but that would not happen. Once again, my "mother imagined" did not materialize.

As we prepared for our son's birth and had our birth plan ready, there were strict instructions not to contact my mother to let her know once I was in labor, nor was she to be in or near the delivery room for obvious reasons. It may sound cruel that we did not want the maternal grandmother to be there, but this was not in any way a loving family situation. She was not happy for me, and we had been estranged for some time, so even just her presence would have caused me additional stress, fear, and trauma. We were certainly going to let her know when the baby was born, but she wasn't on the call list of folks who would be immediately informed.

Our son arrived on a Wednesday night in late July after I had worked almost all day, and the fast delivery had gone perfectly well. My brother started calling folks, and so did my mother-in-law, so our exciting news was spreading fast. When my brother's wife told her mother the good news, her mother then called my mother and told her she should get herself to the hospital right away to see our baby boy, which of course was such a sweet gesture on her part. So my mom came to see us the next day, which was a big surprise. As usual, my Little Girl Self was thrilled and thought maybe she had come around and really did want to be a part of this with us, which of course was not the case. My Big Girl Self was terrified and cautious, not knowing what to expect from her. My mother did hold our son for a few moments while a picture was taken, but that was about it. There was no gushing over me, her daughter, who had just given birth to her only grandchild. She was matter of fact and businesslike in her demeanor, which tells me it was actually very difficult for her to visit us with our new baby. She seems to struggle immensely when we are experiencing happiness, which really makes me sick.

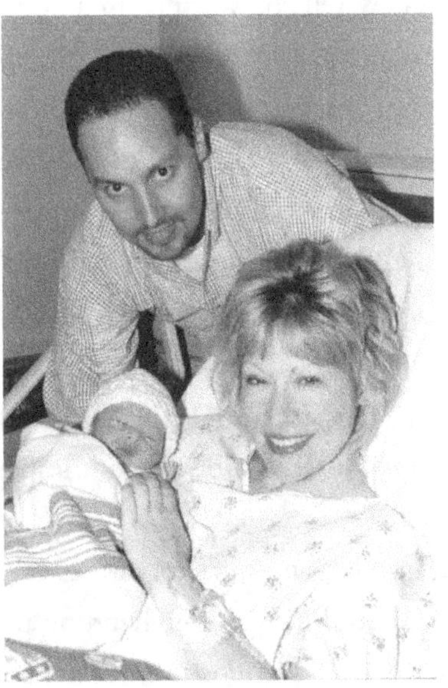

THE NIGHT BLAKE WAS BORN, JULY 27, 2005

Once we were back at home, my mom and stepdad made one quick visit, and they brought us some food as well, which was nice but also customary as part of traditional southern culture, so I think it was more a gesture born of duty rather than genuine joy over our newborn baby boy. Then a few months went by, and my mom's next visit was in early October, after I had been asking her over and over again to come see our precious little one. After all, it was usually me who was always trying to arrange visits and coordinate family connections, thinking that it might also be important to her. My "mother imagined" would have been beside herself trying to get to our house to visit her first and only grandchild. When my mother arrived that day, I could immediately tell she was not in a good state, as my finely tuned radar was very adept at reading her signals after many years of her craziness. She was punchy and short tempered, she did not hug us upon entering the house, and it didn't appear that she wanted to be there at all, which is an interesting observation now that I look back on this painful memory. So why did she even go? Did she visit us out of a feeling of obligation, or maybe just to respond to my continued requests that she visit so I would stop asking? I will never know at this point, and it's impossible for me to rationalize.

We were in our son's nursery, and I was rocking him as Terry stood behind us with one hand on the back of the rocker. My mom stood opposite us and just glared at us with that all-too-familiar look of contempt that I'd seen so often in my life. Of course my "mother imagined" would have immediately held the baby and hugged us both tight as she cooed over our precious baby boy, but that's not what was happening here. She started to talk about my father and how he wasn't any help to her when she had her babies, and I remember feeling so stressed and just praying she would redirect herself before she went any further. Then she said in the most hateful tone, "Your father never stood lovingly over me as I rocked you when you were a baby," and my son started to cry. The tension in the room was palpable, and I was just so exasperated with her. She was acting as if she was enraged at me, which made no sense to me at all. Why in the world had she come to visit us? Just to shut me up? Or maybe so she could tell her relatives that she had been to visit her new grandson again? It simply made no sense.

My husband asked her to leave, and like an idiot I ran out of the front door after her shouting, "Mom, please don't go," and begging her to stay as she walked quickly to her car and completely ignored me. I feel like such a fool when I look back at that memory; it makes me sick to think I was that emotional and fragile. Truly the kid in me, my Little Girl Self, just wanted her mom to love her and experience her new baby, but alas, something that simple and inherent for most humankind was impossible for my mother. We were once again left feeling so confused by her behavior; it was beyond exhausting.

TERRY TOOK THIS PICTURE OF BLAKE AND ME,
NOVEMBER 2005

Over the next several months, I would leave a note with baby pictures enclosed on her windshield in the parking deck where we both parked our cars on weekdays. She never even opened them, and I don't have sufficient words to describe how badly that hurt me. I would find the unopened envelope under my windshield the next day, and I felt so devastated over and over again. I felt abandoned by her, and it just cut like a knife, making me cry again. Obviously she was very angry, but I couldn't understand why she wouldn't want to reconnect or make amends, or how about just keep the pictures of her grandson?

This painful excerpt from my journal reminds me of how I felt as my son's first birthday was approaching; I wrote it on July 3, 2006 (my mom's birthday), and we were estranged again during this time:

Mom turned 60 today, and I didn't call or send a card because I know she'd not answer and she'd send any card back unopened, or better yet, leave it on my windshield in the parking deck that we share, most unfortunately.

She hasn't seen Blake, or us for that matter, since Oct. 2, 2005.

I really hate her for all of the crap she's put us through—she's so cruel and abusive. She has burned many bridges.

I can't believe she doesn't know my precious son and doesn't appear to give a damn about him.

She is a sick, sick woman. I wish she would evaporate.

CHAPTER SEVEN

My Adult to Middle-Age Years

I was often looking for things that might bring my mom some joy, like surprising her with little presents, or showing her random acts of kindness that I thought might brighten her day. At one time she collected any sort of pig decor, so I would always be on the lookout for cute pig gifts for her. She and I shared a love for antiques and old family photos, and in the early 2000s, I discovered a magazine called *Reminisce* (published 1992–2017) that focused on American life in the 1930s through the 1960s. I just knew she'd love it, so I bought her a subscription, as well as one for her elderly aunt in Georgia, whom she dearly loved, and one for myself. It seemed to me that it would be something fun for the three of us to enjoy, and I thought she and her aunt could talk about each issue when they spoke by phone.

After a few months, I noticed that I had not received my *Reminisce* magazine in a while, so I called the publisher to inquire. What I learned was so shocking to me, and truly there are no words to accurately describe how betrayed I felt by my mother's underhanded actions. The representative I spoke with told me there were notes in my file detailing a recent conversation where I was belligerent and angry, requiring them to cancel my three subscriptions right away. Their notes also said they were not to speak with me since I had been so difficult to deal with! Holy cow. I remember actually feeling lightheaded when the representative was telling me this, and I suddenly realized what had happened. Apparently my mother had called them to cancel her subscription, and they thought she was me, thus canceling all three of my subscriptions without providing any refund or voucher for future magazines, and without notifying me, oddly enough. I was completely appalled, and in that moment I told the lady on the phone that my mother is mentally unstable and must have called impersonating me, because I had not ever called them before. The lady responded to me with kindness and said she'd make a note of it in their records. When I asked my mother about it later, she simply said that she no longer wanted the magazine because she didn't want stacks of them sitting around her house, which is ironic to me since she has every single *Southern Living* magazine she's ever received, as well as many others she refuses to get rid of. We did not discuss what I had learned from the publisher about her terrible behavior; I knew better than to bring that up with her as that would be a no-win situation. There is no way to revisit or resolve anything with my mother; she will only argue and foster more anger in every situation.

The year after our son was born, my stepdad was diagnosed with stomach cancer. It was such a difficult time for me because I felt cut off from him by default since my mother and I were estranged yet again. I felt so helpless because I didn't feel comfortable stopping by to see him, and I thought if I mailed him a note, my mother would likely just throw it away in anger. Once I even emailed my stepsister (his daughter), who worked in the same building as I, to ask if she would hand-deliver a note to him the next time she was there to see him. To my great disappointment, she replied that she "didn't want to get in the middle of whatever was going on with my mom and me." And there it is, that grossly incorrect assumption that the situation with my mom is just typical mother-daughter tension or some recent argument between us. I can't tell you how much I want to howl at the moon like a lunatic when people think that's the situation here. This is not about my mom and me or our semblance of a relationship. It's about my mom, her emotional instability, and her obvious yet undiagnosed psychological issues. Learning that my stepsister wouldn't help me was deeply disappointing and made me realize how little she knew about what was really going on. Quite frankly it let me know how little she cared to attempt some level of understanding on my behalf. The memory elicits a twinge of pain when I recall it even to this day.

My stepdad passed away January 30, 2008, and my mother didn't even call me to let me know. In fact, no one in the family contacted me, but I realize that's probably because folks assumed my mother certainly would have let me know. I found out when I called my brother, as I often did each week, and he said he and his wife were actually in the car en route to North Carolina from Massachusetts where they lived at the time. I knew there could only be one reason why they'd be making this trip at this time of the year, and my heart sank. To this day I don't know if my brother was going to tell me the sad news, but I have to believe that was his plan. Perhaps I called him before he had the chance to reach out to me, but I really don't know. It's very possible that my mother insisted that he not contact me about it, but usually my brother didn't comply with her demands as he and I were each other's constant confidants and support system.

I had been robbed of the opportunity to visit my sweet stepfather in the last few years of his life, which was so hard to swallow and still makes me sad, but I was certain that he knew how much I loved him and how much I appreciated everything he had done for my brother and me. I had written him a long letter describing my love and gratitude for him before his cancer diagnosis, and I have no reason to believe he didn't receive it. I also know that he was well aware of the situation with my mom and how hard she could be to deal with, and he most certainly knew how much anger she often hurled in my direction because he had been a witness to it himself many times.

After careful consideration and much deliberation, I decided not to attend his funeral because I had not seen my mother in three years, and it was a very volatile situation.

Gosh, that was such a painful decision to make because either way it made me feel awful and appeared to others that I didn't care enough to be there. My brother reported to me later that my stepsister and stepbrother could not believe I wasn't there, and that hurt for sure, but I also know they had no idea what was going on and wouldn't have understood if I had tried to explain. I felt like an absolute outcast and once again felt abandoned by my mother since I wasn't included in the mourning of my stepfather. Even once my mother and I reconnected later, she never mentioned his funeral to me, so this is yet another sad experience where there were no attempts to explain, understand, or resolve the dysfunction. It still pains me to think about it, even fifteen years after his death, and there are so many things I'd like to say to my mother about that time, but I know that opportunity will never come.

Just over a year after my stepdad's death, I was driving to work one morning, and my brother called me on my cell phone. He said to be prepared because he had some shocking news, then he proceeded to tell me that our mother had recently gotten engaged to a physician from Atlanta whose parents had ties to our parents' hometown. It seems they had connected over email and had been corresponding for several months. She was planning to take early retirement and move with him to Georgia; he even gave her a big solitaire diamond that she was already wearing on her left hand. I received this news during our 2005–2009 estrangement, so I had heard nothing from my mother since a few months after my son was born. I didn't know anything about this man, their courtship, or their plans, and I was dumbfounded to know that she was totally fine with leaving North Carolina without even calling me. In her twisted mind and self-centered world, she was going to leave us behind without even seeing her grandson one more time. That was like a punch in the gut to put it mildly, and it left me in a daze as that old familiar feeling of abandonment hit me all over again. My brother had not met this man either, but at least my mom had told him about their engagement and immediate plans.

As fate would have it, we all ended up in Atlanta over the Christmas holidays of 2009. My mother was with her fiancé at his house, and my husband, brother, son, and I were at my dad and stepmom's house for a few days. This meant we were all in Atlanta at the same time but in two different locations. We were hanging out in the kitchen at Dad's house when all of a sudden my brother received a call from Mom. She and I were estranged at that time, so she did not try to reach me. My brother reported that Mom was upset and on her way to the airport, which was strange because she was supposed to be spending Christmas with her new fiancé and his family. Apparently her fiancé had called off their engagement and sent her back home to North Carolina. To this day that's all I know about this weird situation; even during times of some communication my mother never explained any of it. Lucky for her she was able to resume her job as a state employee because they had not yet processed her early-retirement paperwork.

Over the next decade, life continued in a similar pattern as it always had, where I stayed away from my mom, then reached out to reconnect because I always felt guilty since I'm her oldest child and the only female, thus the expected caretaker. Things would go okay, meaning that I would do some amount of walking on eggshells to keep the peace until she was out of control again, which would then drive me to take leave of her and get as far away from her as I possibly could. In time that cycle would start all over again and would repeat itself for as long as I could stand it. As I look back now, I realize that my Little Girl Self was still patiently waiting for her "mother imagined" to surface and was in the mindset that once the stresses of life lessened, perhaps the mother she needed and wanted would actually appear.

During this time my mother did attend one of our son's soccer matches after I contacted her many times and nearly begged her to go. When she arrived, she had one of her dogs with her and barely communicated with us at all. My "mother imagined" would have been happy to attend the soccer match and would have greeted us with a big hug and smile, especially for Blake, her only grandson. Instead she was weird and robotic, and although she said hello to us, she kept her distance out there on the soccer field like she didn't even know us. It was beyond bizarre.

A few years later, when our son had moved on to basketball, I again requested that she attend one of his games, and after much prompting and reminding, she showed up in the gym at our church where his games were held. It was the same type of behavior, however, which was so discouraging because deep down inside I was still trying to figure out why she acted the way she did. Why in the world wasn't she happy to be there with us? My poor brain was so exhausted from trying to figure that out for so long. For my son's sake, I'm glad that my mother came, but it wasn't at all the way I pictured it in my mind of course. My "mother imagined" would have been loving to Terry and me, and especially to Blake, but in reality she acted distant and strange, almost robotic. We invited her to go to lunch with us or stop by our house, but she declined.

In December of 2017, my mother decided to retire from service as a state employee. Her office held a very nice reception in her honor, and Terry and I were there to celebrate with her, as were my stepsister and her husband. Included in this event were hors d'oeuvres, punch, and a table full of presents. My mom seemed to enjoy this gathering and related to folks pleasantly, thank goodness. As was customary for me, I took several pictures so she could view them later and enjoy the good memory. Once back at home, I quickly uploaded the pictures and created for her a custom-made photo book that turned out so beautiful based on what I could see online. I had it shipped directly to her house so she'd receive it as soon as possible, and I couldn't wait until she saw it! I just knew she would be thrilled. Well, a few weeks went by, and I heard nothing from her, so I called to ask, at which time she informed me that she was never going to open it because her retirement was not a celebration in her opinion. I don't have the energy to even begin to explain what may have prompted her to say that, but all I know is that I was crestfallen that she didn't even open the customized gift I had made for her. It was yet another occasion when I completely failed to predict her reaction or understand what was going on in her mind, but it certainly wasn't the first time.

Not long after my mother's retirement, I paid a visit to a local jewelry store that had long since been a landmark in the town where my mom lives and where I was working at the time. I was making small talk with the owners while they prepared my ticket for a ring that needed resizing. I mentioned that I grew up there and that my mom and stepdad were also customers, having had my mother's pearl engagement ring designed and created there in 1985. They immediately made the connection, then the wife of the owner told me that as many times as my mom had been in their shop, she had never mentioned having a daughter. They only knew from their brief conversations that she had a son, my brother. I remember replying with a smile as I felt the familiar sting and replied with something like "Well, now you know my connection to them." I then thanked them and headed back out to my car, as that old familiar feeling of abandonment and shell shock hit me again. It's so hard to explain what I was feeling, but it felt like an out-of-body experience, like I didn't exist at all. I didn't cry, nor did I even feel angry; I just felt so disgusted and wished that I wasn't connected to her at all.

Over the next five years, there would be several occasions when my mother would call or text to ask if she could borrow some money, or if I could share some groceries with her because she didn't have anything to eat. I always responded by doing whatever I could to help, and sometimes when she asked for a loan, I gave her the money and told her it was a gift not to be repaid. I paid her electric bill a few times as a surprise and also as part of my last Christmas present to her in December of 2021. Many times I would leave a full bag of groceries on her front porch on my way to the office in the morning, then she'd text me to tell me I could pick up my reusable bag later that day. On one of those occasions, I arrived to get what I thought would be my empty bag, only to find that almost all of the groceries I had given her were still in the bag. When I called to ask her about it, she told me she no longer liked tuna, which had been a favorite all of her life, and she provided similar excuses for the other items in the bag. I remember driving off feeling like I was in the Twilight Zone again. It was very strange to say the least, and I just couldn't make any sense of it. I realize now that I had reacted to her need by providing some groceries, but essentially my efforts had been rejected. I felt like a marionette whose strings were being manipulated by the puppeteer, my mother.

It's interesting to note that on those occasions when my mother said she had no money to pay her bills or buy some groceries, her dogs always had everything they needed, including expensive dog food and treats, which I noticed in her pantry. In addition, her financial stresses didn't deter her from making regular online purchases from the QVC shopping network either, which made no sense to me. In my opinion, most of these purchases were for items she didn't need, like a $400 professional stew pot that to this day sits unused in its original box in her downstairs storage area called "the junk room." From my point of view, these purchasing trends were irrational. Why would she forego food and other necessities for her own wellbeing, then make such unnecessary purchases while complaining to us that she had no food?

CHAPTER EIGHT

My Periods of Estrangement from Mom

I've come to realize there is no explanation for my mother, and it's critical that I come to terms with that. If indeed she suffers from borderline personality disorder (BPD), or other psychological or personality disorders, it's highly unlikely she will ever seek psychiatric help that could lead to an actual diagnosis and treatment. If she were willing to do that, her life could have been very different, which is so tragic to me. When I attempt to rationalize my mother's behaviors, I believe that most of them stem from real chemical imbalances and psychological disorders that direct her reactions, but my husband believes that's not what guides her. I truly value his opinions of her because he's been by my side for decades and has witnessed multiple incidents led by her crazy reactions. Based on his observations of Mom for over thirty-five years now, he earnestly believes that although she has likely suffered with depression most of her life, she's been controlling and manipulative since childhood. He suggests that her family members and others around her probably pacified her to keep the peace, thus allowing her total control by default. This learned pattern never required her to accept accountability for her own behavior, which of course intensified her belief that nothing is ever her fault. My close friends who know my history tend to agree with my husband, which is interesting and makes me stop and think. To propose that my mother's words and behaviors are intentional and meant to hurt others, especially me, is sickening. How could anyone be that way?

Dr. Sherrie Campbell describes my mother perfectly when she writes, "People with pathological personalities, on the other hand, respond more like regressed, stubborn, vengeful bullies. They are never wrong. They are above apologies. They never question if they could have or should have done anything differently. And everything in their lives is an embellished drama of how they have been victimized by others" (2019, 2). I cannot emphasize enough how true her description is when I think about my mother. It's like the author herself had been a fly on the wall at my house growing up and had witnessed my mom's tantrums and erratic behavior. Wow.

Perhaps Mom has had a psychological disorder since childhood, but it was not dealt with since mental health wasn't discussed as often back in the '50s? I will always wonder about that but will likely not uncover many answers, except that I've learned Mom suffered with extreme anxiety as a child and was also likely depressed. As I look back on the past few decades, I'm reminded that one way for me to deal with her was to just stay away from her. Typically, a new period of estrangement would start like this: I would be with my mom in person or talking with her on the phone, then she would start reprimanding or criticizing me, our conversation would end, and I would not initiate contact for several weeks, months, or even years at a time. I went through countless rounds of estrangement that played out exactly like that, until I decided to get off of the roller coaster for good in the spring of 2022.

As Dr. Campbell so beautifully puts it, "We feel obligated to return to our parents partly because we're trying to make sense of the fact that our own family, especially our mother, does not truly love us" (2019, 106). I wonder if it was this innate obligation that guided me for most of my life to keep returning to my mother to try to make things better. It was incredibly painful when I had the realization that my own mother doesn't love me, and that milestone started a period of mourning for me. It's really difficult to mourn someone who is still living, but that's what was happening to me. I had finally reached the point where I realized the mother I had imagined for decades was not there and never would be. Truly I believe this type of mourning is harder than the kind we feel when someone passes away, because it fools us with the false hope that the person who is still living might get better and reach out to us, but again, that never happens.

Looking back now I realize there were actually many times when I tried to separate myself from my mother, which tells me that I really was aware that I needed to get away from her, even when I was much younger than I am now. These occasions were earnest attempts to set some boundaries with my mother but would instead result in yet another estrangement. Being estranged, however, does not mean any progress toward healing is happening; it simply makes things better because the source of pain and anger is not around for a certain time period. The timeline I created when I started therapy in 2022 has helped me tremendously because it provides concrete documentation of how many times I had separated myself from her:

- August–December 1991
- 1993–1996
- 2003–2005
- 2005–2009
- 2022–present

It's important to note that those are just the times I recorded in my journals; I know there were other times when I just didn't write it down, much to my dismay.

During the 2005–2009 estrangement, when my son was in his first four years of life, my mother actually called the land line at our house on January 24, 2009, but did not leave a message on the answering machine. It's interesting that January 24 was my maternal grandmother's birthday, so I don't know if my mom was prompted to call us because she had spoken with her own mother earlier that day, or what. My husband promptly called her back to inquire what she needed, and she replied that she'd like us to reconcile and "put the past behind us" for a new start in 2009. Terry responded that he would talk with me and let her know. I sent a beautiful card to Mom on February 3 stating that I believe we could make a new start, but much healing must occur, and we'd need to work hard and be patient. After writing her a poetic note about love, patience, self-reflection, and understanding, I signed the card "Let this be a new day, full of promise and endless possibilities." At that time my Little Girl Self was still very much in control and was hoping with all her might for a miraculous personality change.

We talked with my brother and decided that the three of us would go meet with my mother as an informal intervention of sorts, and we paid her a visit on Sunday, February 15, 2009. My brother was planning a visit that day anyway because it was the weekend of our stepdad's birthday, and he had only been gone one year by that point. In my journal I summarized our two-hour discussion with her, and the main point we made is that we want her to see a psychiatrist before we can move forward. Well, she handled things fairly well, but she was aloof and disconnected, and ultimately she said we were the ones with the problem.

The last note I wrote to myself in my journal was this:

We don't expect anything to change. I will NEVER understand WHY.

What is totally different about my most recent estrangement from my mother is that it's the very last one, and I know that I am in control of that decision. When I last saw her on April 14, 2022, and was pulling out of her driveway after being treated like crap once again, I knew it was over. I knew right then and there that I was never going back. It was the straw that broke the camel's back, so to speak, and I knew I had reached a major milestone in this journey. As Stephanie Foo describes, "Really, estrangement is more of a continuum, where you can either be more or less estranged, and actually people often go through multiple times of trying to create distance before they're able to maintain a level of distance that's right for them" (2022, 219). Well, I had just figured out the right "level of distance" for me, and that was as much distance as possible, as in not ever seeing her again.

For my mother, everything is a competition, and all topics are worth arguing about, yet she told me all my life that I myself "would argue with a fencepost." It's now so obvious how much she projected her own issues onto me, her daughter. She was always so critical of me and degraded me at nearly every turn. No matter the person with whom she's talking, she will negate their comments and attempt to outdo them with her own experiences, leaving that person feeling devalued and definitely not heard. From what I've observed and heard, she's had "run-ins" with most of her family members, her work colleagues before she retired, her neighbors, and the few close friends that she has. Mom has been hateful to my brother's best friend from high school when he was there to help her years ago, and she's also been mean to my son, which is simply atrocious and beyond my realm of understanding. Because of that, she's at home much of the time by herself, accompanied only by her dogs, which would seem to be precisely what she wants, yet she often complained about no one coming over to see her. It's so interesting to me that she simply does not make the connection that when you treat people badly, they eventually stop trying, and they stop coming around.

"Estrangement is not freeing. It has not felt joyful. It has not been happy. It has only felt necessary, and even that is something I question all the time" (Foo 2022, 224). In chapter 34 of her book, Foo goes on to describe that removing her toxic parents from her life protected her but did not fix her. "The excision was not healing in and of itself. Instead, it cleared the way for me to rebuild" (Foo 2022, 225). I now understand what she means, and I wholeheartedly agree.

~

CHAPTER NINE

My Last Experience with Mom

On Thursday, April 14, 2022, I drove to my mother's house so we could go to her bank and add me to her accounts like she, my brother, and I had discussed a few years prior. Losing our father in 2018 made us realize that one of us needed to be listed on her accounts so bills could continue to get paid if she was incapacitated for some reason. She insisted that my brother had refused to do this for her, but he insisted that wasn't the case, and I believed him because her reality is often so skewed. Since I had recently retired, I now had the time to go to the bank with her during the week.

Mom had made an eleven o'clock appointment with Truist Bank to get me added to her bank accounts after I had mentioned this to her a few days back when she called me; it was unfinished business from two years ago when my brother and I had just dealt with our father's death. I arrived at her house at twenty-five past ten, and she had just stepped out of the shower; she was in a towel, and her hair was wet. Her demeanor was not at all friendly, and she actually seemed agitated. She reluctantly gave me a half hug when I reached out to do so as I always do when I enter her house. She told me that she'd be ready in time and for me to sit in the kitchen and wait for her to get dressed. I now realize that her signals to me were about her feeling like I was demanding that she do this, which was not the case. My brother and I had made this suggestion to her a few years ago, but we had simply not made it happen yet, so I thought I was helping.

We arrived at the bank right before eleven o'clock, and a friendly gentleman named Michael helped us. Mom was fine, albeit very punchy, and did say at one point that her kids are "afraid she'll croak soon" and wanted to make sure one of us was on her accounts just in case. She told Michael that her son "doesn't want any part of this," which is why I was there, thus making a point that I was not her first choice. Michael seemed to sense the tension but remained professional and friendly as he tried to complete the process for her. She was insistent that my name not appear on her checks or accounts, and Michael said that was easy to set up, that it would appear in the background only for staff, so they'd know I was approved to make deposits or write checks. She had a few more unrelated questions that he addressed, then we left.

We were back in the car before eleven thirty, so I suggested we go to Subway for lunch (my treat as always), but we never got that far. She got riled up and started telling me in her hateful tone that she sure is happy she could accommodate my schedule to get this done, and of course it went downhill from there. Another "turn" was coming for sure.

She mentioned the fallout with my brother and his wife from over a year ago when there had been a phone conversation between her and my brother, and he had her on speakerphone. During their conversation she referred to my sister-in-law as a "slut," which then prompted my sister-in-law to reply with "Kiss my ass." Mom loved to rehash negative experiences over and over again, and she also liked picking fights in my opinion, but I'm not sure why she brought this up to me again at this time. I offered up some additional insight but told her I understood if she didn't believe me or didn't want to hear it. She then told me she didn't ask for my opinion, and I told her that she was the one who brought it up, and I was the only one in the car, so why did she even bring it up? I told her I didn't want to rehash it again because it wouldn't change the outcome, and it always left me in a bad mood. This was very out of character for me because up until now, I just suffered through her ranting again and again as she treated me like a scolded child. She became infuriated and told me I could not control what she thought and said, and she would discuss whatever she wanted to discuss.

It's important to note that this was likely the very first time I had ever really stood up to my mother. It was quite possibly my initial attempt to set a real boundary with her, so it was a big milestone in my recovery and healing process.

Stephanie Foo describes a similar experience with her own mother by saying, "For the first time, the power balance between me and my mother had shifted" (2022, 27). This of course was infuriating to my mother and left me feeling tense and afraid, as always. As she glared at me from the passenger seat, the tension was palpable. I honestly felt like I didn't even know who was riding in the car with me.

At this point she angrily demanded that I turn around and take her home, and that she did not want any lunch. It was obvious she was irate and wanted no part of being with me, not that she had wanted to be with me that day to begin with. As I drove the short distance from there to her house, she told me in her mean and cutthroat tone that she was tired of my always trying to control her by not allowing her to talk about certain things, and she again described a few specifics about the falling out she had with my brother and his wife. Once in her driveway, she glared at me with her dark eyes and said that she didn't trust me and "doesn't want to do business with me." This last statement from her was bizarre to me, and to this day I'm not sure what she meant by it.

Her face looked physically different, like she was someone else entirely, and she was absolutely livid. I replied by saying that was a horrible thing to say to me since I thought I was helping her by coming today, and she said, "I don't care. You've treated me so badly for most of my life," and got out of the car. Wow—that was it. I remember thinking to myself, surely if God is in His Heaven, He will send down a lightning bolt to evaporate her right now. The irony of what she said was so cruel, there are no words to describe it. I drove off feeling shell shocked and dazed, not even comprehending what had just transpired. Before long I had driven about ten miles south and called my husband from a parking lot; I didn't even remember how I had arrived there. My therapist explained that this feeling I experience after such negative incidents with my mother is actually a form of posttraumatic stress disorder, or PTSD. She has also told me that I've likely experienced complex PTSD (CPTSD) due to the frequency and nature of these traumatic interactions with my mother.

It's interesting to note that in the year prior to this last "turn" from my mother, I had helped her through two surgeries: one for a thumb joint replacement (4/23/21) and one for kidney stones (8/4/21). I also helped her with an outpatient series of spinal injections. In each of these incidents, she had asked me in advance if I could help her, which of course I agreed to do, being her dutiful daughter. I took time off of work, drove her to the hospital and back home again, stayed at her house to take care of her dogs, made sure she had meals and her medications, and did anything she needed me to do without question. During these times she was very loving to me and almost giddy to see me. She was wonderful to the nurses, and they all commented on what a sweet person she was and that she must be a terrific mother. Boy, it was hard for me not to roll my eyes like an angry teenager when I heard their comments, but of course I did the southern ladylike thing and smiled graciously, thanking them for what they had all done for my mom. After the surgery for her kidney stones, the surgeon came out to talk to me and said, "Boy, your mother is a real pill," to which I responded, "You don't know the half of it." It was actually a rare moment of humor that also provided a small bit of validation for me.

The last "turn" from my mother in April of 2022 was to be the beginning of my complete and final separation from her, my choice for a "no contact" relationship, as Dr. Sherrie Campbell calls it. There would be no turning back after this last incident with her. It is a gross understatement to say that I was completely done with this insane roller coaster I'd been riding for over forty years. As Stephanie Foo so eloquently describes it, "Something inside me closed toward her that would never open again" (2022, 27). I knew just as soon as I pulled out of my mother's driveway that day that it would be the last time. The weight of that primal feeling takes time to digest and is difficult to describe. Once again I was completely shell-shocked as I drove almost ten miles without an awareness of where I was going. The old familiar sting was back, and in a daze my instincts led me to simply get away from her. I felt so disillusioned by what had transpired, and as always, I just didn't understand. My "mother imagined" would have appreciated my efforts earlier that day, but in her usual pattern, my actual mother responded with anger and hate.

CHAPTER TEN

My Happy Memories

As I reflect on the last four decades of my life since adolescence, I do have some memories of happy times with my mom, and of course I cherish them, although I know they do not represent a realistic picture of her. Most of the time my mother was angry and stressed, and her outlook on life was usually very pessimistic. Out of every ten experiences with her, eight would vary from negative to horrible, and two would be decent or good. I now believe that perhaps it would have been better for me if she had been awful all of the time so I wouldn't have hung on to the false hope that those few good times provided.

When I was in the fifth grade and we still lived in our townhouse, I returned home from school one day to find a beautiful brand-new Laura Ashley comforter and shams (plum and cream colors) on my antique brass bed, as well as lovely ruffled curtains my mom had actually custom-designed and hand-sewn herself. I was ecstatic and felt like a princess! There was no specific occasion; it was just a nice thing my mother did for me out of the blue, and I remember feeling absolutely overjoyed. I was so proud of my room's new look, and I made my bed every single day so I could enjoy its beauty each afternoon after school.

Around that same time, I woke up in the middle of the night to find my mother sitting at the dining room table eating Reese's peanut butter cups. I think I was actually sleepwalking, but when I found Mom there, I sat with her, and we both ate Reese's together. She didn't seem angry that I was up in the middle of the night, and I actually felt welcome to join her at the table. I remember it being a quiet and relaxed time with no stress while my dad and brother were asleep upstairs in their beds. She wasn't bothered in the least that I was out of my bed and interrupting her quiet time. We just sat together and quietly enjoyed the Reese's.

In upper elementary and junior high years, my friends and I loved to go roller skating at the local skating rink that had a smooth fiberglass floor. My brother often joined us, and it was a favorite pastime for all of us. Sometimes my mother joined us, which was really cool, and I quickly learned what an accomplished skater she was. I remember not feeling embarrassed at all, which of course was atypical of a kid that age. Instead, I felt proud that my mom could get out there and skate with all of those teenagers. She really enjoyed herself and smiled a lot while she was skating, which was wonderful to see and made me feel happy.

While we still lived in the townhouse and my dad had not yet moved out, the movie *History of the World, Part I*

(1981) came on TV through our new Time Warner cable subscription, and we watched it together as a family. One of the characters (played by Mel Brooks) mentions a "piss bucket," which launched my mom into hysterics that continued for several minutes. She was rolling around on the living room carpet laughing so hard that she could barely breathe. Very soon all four of us were cackling, even though my brother and I didn't really understand what was so funny; it was just so unusual to see Mom dying laughing like that. It still makes me smile when I recall that comical time and happy memory. I have no memory of my mom ever laughing like that again, which is really sad.

After Mom married my stepdad and we lived at his house, I remember a time when the radio was on, and my mother and I were both in the kitchen in our socks. The song "You Got the Best of My Love," by The Emotions (1977), came on, and it was one of our very favorite songs. We both danced like crazy fools all over the kitchen floor as we sang along to the lyrics and did "the bump" with each other as the music played. It was so much fun and allowed me a rare glimpse of the fun and spunky side of my mother. I remember that occasion fondly every time I hear that old song.

When I was in high school, I remember one really busy morning when I needed a shirt ironed but was running behind and feeling very stressed. Mom came to my rescue and ironed my shirt, and I felt so relieved by her gesture. It made me happy to know that she earnestly wanted to help me, and it actually seemed to bring her joy, which made me feel loved by my mother.

During my sophomore year in college, I had all four wisdom teeth removed, and Mom was the perfect helper and nurse. She drove me to my appointment, got my prescriptions after the surgery, took me home, and set me up in my room with my black-and-white TV and pillows to prop me up, so I was well taken care of. I remember feeling loved and doted upon by her during that recovery. She was always a terrific nurse if any of us were sick or recovering; it was when she would really shine.

During my junior year in college, my mom showed up in my dorm and surprised me with a white teddy bear, twenty-one yellow roses (my favorite color rose), and a watch that had floating crystals inside the face for my twenty-first birthday. Her visit was so unexpected, and it was just wonderful. She wished me happy birthday and gave me a hug, which left me feeling overjoyed with a big smile on my face right there in my college dormitory.

My thirtieth birthday in 1999 found me in a night class during graduate school, which was a major bummer for sure. When class ended and I arrived at my car, my mom was waiting there with all of my favorites: homemade tuna salad, unsweet tea, and a Diet Coke. Wow! She had surprised me on my thirtieth birthday, which was so unexpected and wonderful. Her demeanor was very matter of fact and businesslike, but she had made the effort to wish me a happy birthday on my thirtieth birthday, which I thought was terrific. I savored that experience all the way home as I enjoyed the goodies she brought me.

Throughout my young-adult and older-adult years, my mother would often brag about me when I was with her and we ran into a friend or colleague in person, which actually surprised me. She would talk about my Spanish speaking ability, and also about the awards and recognitions I'd received during my teaching career. It was really nice to experience, but her behavior toward me when others weren't around was the absolute polar opposite. This dichotomy made me distrust the times when she bragged about me and acted as if she were proud of me.

Words cannot express how much I treasure these good memories with my mom, because in truth the happy times were very few, especially after my early childhood once we had settled in North Carolina. The difficulty is that on each of these "good" occasions, the unexpected and unusual positive tone deceived me because I thought maybe she was "getting better" or "getting over" whatever it was that had always bothered her. My Little Girl Self relished the thought that maybe Mom would soon be the fairy tale Mom she (I myself) had always pictured in her mind, the "mother imagined," but of course it was not to be.

CHAPTER ELEVEN

My Healing Journey

I have written my story and have put some memories down on paper, or at least some of the most relevant ones. There are literally hundreds of other related stories about dealing with my mother, but it would take me a life-time to record and explain all of them. Some of them I only remember bits and pieces of anyway, and others would require more energy than I'm willing to expend if I were to make an attempt at including them in this book. What I have written here, therefore, is but a snapshot of the entire story. The important thing is that I am healing, and I have finally separated myself from my toxic mother, both physically and emotionally. I will continue to work with my therapist for some time as I strive to understand past trauma with my mother, as well as my past and future reactions to that trauma and related experiences. As Sherrie Campbell so beautifully puts it, "For any change in the dysfunctional relationship to occur, the pressure is on us to change our pattern of letting them seep back into our lives. We have to change our pattern to one of strict and unbendable boundaries no matter how seductive their ploys are to suck us back in" (2019, 106). I have begun to change the dysfunctional patterns of which I've been a part by default all of my life.

It's hard to say when my healing journey actually began, although there are significant conversations and realizations that were part of my journey even before I ever sought professional therapy in 2022. Perhaps the most memorable is having dinner with a dear friend when we were both out of town at an educators' conference held in Wilmington, North Carolina, in the early 2000s when I was in my early thirties. I was sharing with her a situation involving my mother and was trying to define my very complicated maternal relationship, when my friend suddenly said, "You know you were abused, right?" She went on to explain that my relationship with my mom was not normal and has obviously been detrimental to me. To say that I was astounded is a severe understatement; I was actually speechless for a few moments as I let her informal analysis sink in.

Believe it or not, I had not yet considered the relationship with my mother as abusive or toxic, although it most certainly was and had been for many years. I was still deep inside of that dysfunctional cycle of justifying my mother's behaviors and hoping for improvement over and over again. At that time, I couldn't yet see the situation for what it actually was: a toxic mother whose anger, unpredictable moods, and wrath had been aimed at me for decades. This unexpected conversation with my friend was pivotal for me and was likely the true beginning of my healing journey. That monumental event was over twenty years ago now, which is hard to believe.

When I fast forward to the present day as I'm in therapy, it's important to mention that my therapist taught me to continue delineating my Little Girl Self and Big Girl Self as I seek to understand my own reactions and emotions involving my mother. She reminds me to let my Big Girl Self take the lead and guide me as I process my thoughts, memories, and emotions. She also reminds me that my Little Girl Self will continue to have her own feelings and reactions, which I must recognize and not disregard. I now realize that in my dinner conversation with my dear friend over twenty years ago, my Little Girl Self was in charge and managing my thoughts at the time and would continue to do so for many more years. My Little Girl Self still seeks a caring mother who loves and responds the way one would expect, so it is she who feels intense waves of sadness at certain unexpected times, but my Big Girl Self nonetheless understands this dynamic and remains diligent as these emotions come.

For decades I had ridden that repetitive emotional roller coaster that went something like this: I reached out to my mom, things went okay because I pacified her, then she would suddenly explode at me, which usually resulted in my staying away from her for some period of time. As Christine Lawson explains, adult children like me "never know from one minute to the next how their mother feels about them; the mother's moods can suddenly change from affection to rage, creating an uncertain and insecure emotional environment" (2000, 7). For me these occurrences resulted in periods of estrangement ranging from a few weeks to as long as four years. The timeline I shared in chapter 8, which I created during the first few months of therapy, has shown me in black and white just how many times we were estranged, and it's quite eye-opening to see. These are just the times I chose to record in my journals, though, so I know it's not an exhaustive list and doesn't show a complete account of my estrangements from her.

I realize now that it was always me reaching out to her, even once my son, her only grandson, was born; it was never the other way around unless she needed something from me like money, groceries, or help with a medical procedure. I was always trying to communicate with her and spend time with her, but my efforts were never reciprocated. I understand now that she actually did not want to be around me, no matter what I did or said, which is very painful to accept. "We erroneously believe that if we try to be good enough, successful, or perfect, maybe our toxic family members will change their minds about us. But they don't and they won't" (Campbell 2019, 107).

My mother used to call me on the phone often, but she wasn't reaching out to check on me and my family. She would trap me for well over an hour rehashing the same angry stories from ancient family history, much to my dismay. She often recounted her separation and divorce from my dad, even though she had told those stories hundreds of times. I didn't understand why she was still retelling them after decades had passed, and even after my dad's death in 2018. Interestingly enough, when she called me, she never once asked me how I was doing, or how things were going for me or my family. Alas she was only calling to express her disgust about something or someone, or rake me over the coals for God only knows what, or to describe a litany of medical issues and test results with a disgusted tone in her voice as if I were to blame. She has not ever apologized to me, even after saying horrible and hurtful things to me, nor has she ever admitted that she was mistaken or made any errors in judgment. There were multiple occasions that warranted a sincere apology to me or to someone else, but those apologies never happened since my mother believes that the rest of the world is to blame.

Working with my therapist has taught me a lot, but one very important lesson I've learned is to actually experience my own feelings when they occur, rather than pushing them aside or ignoring them. In other words, the goal is to allow myself to go through what I'm feeling instead of trying to reason with it, justify it, blame myself for it, or sugarcoat it. I realize that we are innately programmed to figure things out and make sense of what we experience in life, and our brains will repeatedly guide us to do just that. This is particularly hard for me because I'm trying to rewire my brain where my mom is concerned. For years I have tried to understand why she is the way she is and have constantly sought reasons for her behaviors, all while honestly believing that maybe one day she would change. In every difficult situation that involves my mom, the common denominator is always her, without exception. This process of acknowledging my own emotional state is very difficult for me and something I am only just beginning to learn. "Talking gives us knowledge about why we are the way we are, but that knowledge isn't enough. Processing, on the other hand, allows us to truly come to terms with our trauma and resolve it—to rewrite the memories in our brains with a healthier narrative" (Foo 2022, 98).

In cultures around the world, there is an expectation for adult children to care for their aging parents, although there are varying degrees of this expectation based on many factors. In southern American culture, it's both an expectation and a duty with a direct connection to the Book of Exodus in the Holy Bible, where it says, "Honor thy father and thy mother" (Exodus 20:12). I've struggled immensely with this concept all of my adult life, and I cringe when I'm at family gatherings and hear someone mention that we owe our parents this type of love and care because I simply cannot reconcile it with my own situation. I do realize that honoring one's parents can mean many different things, but I'm still working through my feelings of guilt, fear, and confusion where this concept is concerned. It's a fact that I will not care for my mother in her old age since I have chosen to have no contact with her. When I think about that, I feel like I'm dishonoring her, but for me it's just too toxic and damaging to even consider. My dear friend, who talked with me over twenty years ago in Wilmington, recently told me that she believes I'm actually honoring my mother by staying away from her and no longer enabling her toxic behavior. If I were to reach out to my mother again for any reason, it would be like a recovering alcoholic taking a shot of whiskey and throwing years of sobriety out the window in an instant. This is what I keep telling myself as I struggle with this biblical directive to those of us who have faith, but it remains very difficult for me.

Over the past four decades, I've always felt like I had to defend my mom whenever my dad's side of the family asked about her, especially once my parents separated in December of 1982. I would answer with factual information but would really emphasize anything positive and never mention anything negative or the craziness we were experiencing. I would respond like, "Oh, she's fine. She's busy with work and taking care of her dogs." It was the socially acceptable response that provided a basic answer to their question, but it didn't allow me to share any of the traumatic experiences that were happening or open up to seek support. My Little Girl Self has always wanted to point out the very best things about her and protect her reputation, especially with my dad's family. My Big Girl Self, however, wants vehemently to shout from the rooftops how truly awful she has been to me, and how I never want to lay eyes on her again. I could shout out a litany of things my mother has done that are totally contrary to what mothers should do, but alas, that will only happen in my fantasy world.

The most meaningful part of my healing journey has been the validation I've received from family members, namely my mother's sister, Jane, and my mother's brother, Mike. The first time I ever shared any bits of truth about my mother with her family was at my Aunt Jane's house in 2007 when I was there to attend my cousin's wedding in Atlanta. I had just started reading *Understanding The Borderline Mother* by Christine Lawson, and it nearly took my breath away how close to home it was for me. I literally felt like I couldn't breathe as I finished the first chapter. I started sharing some surface-level information with my mom's sister to test the waters so to speak. It was so helpful just to begin opening up a tiny bit with someone who knew my mother well, and thankfully my aunt seemed to welcome it. Since that time at my aunt's house in 2007, I've been sharing stories and experiences with her from time to time, as well as with Uncle Mike, who is my mom's younger brother and also a retired psychologist. Honestly, I've shared more with my mom's two siblings over the past five years than ever before, and every time I divulge another story about my mother, I feel more weight lifted from my shoulders. I know for a fact that I could not have experienced the progress I've made without their constant love, support, and validation.

Starting to open up to my mom's two siblings was a big milestone in and of itself, but deciding when and how to share any amount of my truth with my dad's family was altogether different and weighed on me heavily. After all, this was the side of the family Mom saw as her enemy after the divorce, even though she had attended school with my dad's younger siblings, and they all knew each other. I talked at length with my therapist and brainstormed suitable responses that would allow me to be honest without ripping my mother to shreds, providing unnecessary details, or regurgitating horrible experiences to my unassuming relatives. We decided that I could say, "I wish I knew," when folks asked about my mother, and that it would also be totally appropriate for me to say, "I haven't heard from her in a while." My therapist and I discussed other possibilities as I began to prepare mentally for my next trip to my parents' hometown.

In January of 2024, my dad's older brother passed away. He was the oldest of the six siblings and had been the patriarch of the family since my paternal grandmother died in 2008. I traveled down to southwest Georgia to be with my dad's side of the family, and it was during this time that I began to answer honestly when folks asked about my mother. It was a major coming out for me; it was the most courageous step yet in the milestones of my healing journey. A friend of the family asked me how my mom was doing, and I replied calmly that I no longer communicate with her, surprising myself as the words left my mouth. Wow—I actually said it! My decades-long secret was now out in the open among my dad's family. A little while later, an uncle also asked me about my mother, and I replied with the same response I had given to the other lady earlier. My uncle then asked me what I thought was wrong with her, which let me know that he was more aware of her issues than I thought. After all, he and his siblings grew up in the same town as my mother and attended the same school, so perhaps my relatives actually knew my mother better than I ever realized.

My birthday, my mother's birthday, and holidays are difficult and likely always will be because of what my Little Girl Self expects and wants to do, and what my Big Girl Self knows isn't possible or would be unhealthy. Mother's Day is especially grueling since it brings about an array of emotions that are extremely difficult to process, even as the years go by and even though I myself am a mother. I dread its approach every spring without exception. The sappy-sweet cards describing a mother's constant love and devotion literally nauseate me because they are so very far removed from my particular situation with my mother. With the help of my therapist, I've learned that I simply have to face these occasions and keep moving forward without dwelling on the movie of what could have been that plays again and again in my mind. I try to focus instead on my husband and my son, my other family members, and my dear friends and colleagues. When Mother's Day passes again each year, I am tremendously relieved that I won't face it again for another twelve months.

It breaks my heart that my own mother is not in my life and almost never reaches out to my son, her only grandchild, but it is what it is, as they say. I cannot fix it, nor can I even improve it. I have realized that my last option was what Dr. Sherrie Campbell calls the "no contact option," which involves setting up a permanent boundary, so to speak, to protect myself and move forward without my mother's constant criticism and verbal assaults. I no longer reach out to her, and I keep myself completely separate from her, which has helped me begin a path to genuine healing. It's not the natural way of things, and without a doubt it's not what I wanted for my life, but it's the reality in front of me that I must face. It has been a difficult path filled with all levels of emotion and a good amount of guilt because I'm her oldest child and her only daughter, but it was the path I needed to take.

In late November of 2023, I dreamed about writing a book, and I even awoke with the title in my mind like someone had written it just for me: *Mother Imagined*. It came to me like some sort of divine inspiration out of the blue, so I figured maybe it was a sign from God. It's not something I had ever considered before, but I realized it might be beneficial as I continue my healing journey, so I captured some of my life experiences in black and white. The words flowed, and I couldn't type fast enough to keep up. Eleven chapters surfaced in no time, and here we are. It reminded me of Forrest in the *Forrest Gump* movie, where he ran great distances all over the country, then one day just stopped because he had simply finished running.

I want to thank my small group of close girlfriends, who were very supportive of me in junior high school and on into high school, college, and beyond. We remain dear friends to this very day, and I hope my acknowledgement of them in the dedication of this book reminds them of how very grateful I am. They will occasionally mention issues with my mom from years ago that I had filed in the back of my mind and had not yet retrieved. On those occasions, I am sometimes surprised at what I don't remember or had not thought about in many years. In the midst of my current healing journey at middle age, remembering these situations and looking at them with a new lens is very healthy for me. It's an important reminder to myself to celebrate all that I've accomplished thus far on this healing journey. I'm so thankful to my friends for always being there without fail.

I wish all the best for my mother and truly hold no ill will toward her, but I no longer cling to the false hope that we will ever connect or have a normal relationship. I know beyond a shadow of a doubt that it would be detrimental to my own well-being to continue reaching out to her or trying to establish some sort of relationship. Alas, my "mother imagined" is just a figure held in my heart and my mind that isn't a real person at all. My actual mother isn't capable of being the kind of mother I've always wanted and needed, and I realize that now. She has some serious issues that have never been realized or addressed to my knowledge, and based on my experiences with her, she isn't likely to seek any form of professional help. Sometimes it still hits me hard for no apparent reason, but I do my best to work through the heavy feelings until they pass yet again, which is something my therapist has taught me. I try to remember that my Little Girl Self will often start to miss her "mother imagined," and the intense sadness creeps back in to overwhelm me like a heavy fog, but my Big Girl Self then takes the lead to put the pieces back together, get me back on track, and let some sunshine in once again.

My task at this point in my life is to continue making progress in my healing journey and just keep moving forward one step at a time. I sincerely hope that the reflections I have written from my own personal experiences will somehow benefit others who find themselves in a similar situation with a toxic parent and who choose to read my story.

WITH BLAKE AND TERRY, AUGUST 2021

References

Campbell, Sherrie. 2019. *But It's Your Family…: Cutting Ties with Toxic Family Members and Loving Yourself in the Aftermath.* New York: Morgan James.

Foo, Stephanie. 2022. *What My Bones Know: A Memoir of Healing from Complex Trauma.* New York: Ballantine Books.

Lawson, Christine Ann. 2000. *Understanding The Borderline Mother.* Lanham, Maryland: Rowman & Littlefield.

Mason, Paul T., and Randi Kreger. 2010. *Stop Walking on Eggshells.* 2nd ed. Oakland, California: New Harbinger.

About the Author

Reason Carmichael, a Florida-born, North Carolina-raised author, holds a B.A. and M.Ed. from Meredith College, Raleigh. Her extensive career in education spans roles as a high school teacher, a central office administrator, and education consultant at the state level. Carmichael's personal life is marked by a happy marriage of over thirty years and a son who is now in college. Residing a short drive south of Raleigh, she brings her rich life experiences into her writing. Her book, Mother Imagined, reflects her understanding of complex familial relationships, resonating with adults who've experienced toxic relationships with parents or guardians.